Reading Contemporary African American Literature

Reading Contemporary African American Literature

Black Women's Popular Fiction, Post–Civil Rights Experience, and the African American Canon

Beauty Bragg

LEXINGTON BOOKS
Lanham • Boulder • New York • London

Published by Lexington Books
An imprint of The Rowman & Littlefield Publishing Group, Inc.
4501 Forbes Boulevard, Suite 200, Lanham, Maryland 20706
www.rowman.com

Unit A, Whitacre Mews, 26-34 Stannary Street, London SE11 4AB

British Library Cataloguing in Publication Information Available

Library of Congress Cataloging-in-Publication Data
Bragg, Beauty, 1969-
Reading contemporary African American literature : Black women's popular fiction, post-civil rights
experience, and the African American canon / Beauty Bragg.
p. cm.
Includes bibliographical references and index.
ISBN 978-0-7391-8878-1 (cloth) — ISBN 978-0-7391-8879-8 (ebook) 1. American literature—
African American authors. 2. American literature—Women writers. I. Title.
PS508.N3B67 2015
810.9'896073—dc23
2014034422
ISBN 978-1-4985-0714-1 (pbk)

 TM

Contents

Acknowledgments

While writing this book, I have benefitted from the support of many friends and colleagues. At Georgia College, Bruce Gentry, Sandra Godwin, Esther Lopez, Katie Simon, and Mark Vail provided support and encouragement. The Office of Academic Affairs gave much needed time away from my teaching duties in the form of a Faculty Research Leave. My department chair, Elaine Whitaker, too, has been generous in her support of various development activities which fed into this project.

Although we write in solitude, the work we do is not improved by isolation. Thanks to the anonymous reviewer who provided valuable feedback. The National Women's Studies Association and the 2012 NEH Institute on Contemporary African American literature have been invaluable sources of intellectual community. In these spaces I cultivated relationships with Heidi Lewis, Jennifer Freeman-Marshall, Kameelah Martin, Thabiti Lewis, Ayesha Hardison, and many others, which have sustained me intellectually and spiritually. I also need to acknowledge the invaluable contributions of another network of supporters who helped me to keep my eye on the ball: Tayari Jones, Michele Reid-Vazquez, Van Garrett, and Pancho McFarland were always available, in person or via telephone, to help raise my spirits and remind me of the importance of my work.

Finally, I want to thank my sons, Salvador and Malik, and my mother, Mary Anderson. Their love, laughter, and help with fulfilling the obligations of day-to-day life made it possible for me to give this project the attention it required.

Introduction

Locating an African American Literary Tradition

My interest in the work of popular African American women writers is rooted in my experience with students for whom the term "African American literature" largely means popular literature. Such students—English majors and non-majors with an interest in Black Studies—have not had much exposure to the "classics" of African American literature. Having come of age in a largely integrated (and structurally racist) environment, their exposure to "literature" has focused on a Eurocentric tradition with, perhaps, a tokenistic nod to Langston Hughes. Added to that, the fact that their informal encounters with African American literature (or fiction, if you must) were likely to be primarily shaped by a consumer market which, naturally, promotes a highly commercial form, means that their notions of African American literature and mine differ significantly.

After having the repeated experience of missed connections with students who couldn't believe that I had not read Zane's *Addicted* or Sapphire's *Push*—which they were relating to texts like *Sula* or *The Bluest Eye*—I began to include such material in my own leisure reading. Finally, beginning with Sistah Souljah's *The Coldest Winter Ever*, I began to incorporate the occasional urban fiction title in my courses. As I attempted to incorporate a wider variety of titles—some of which were much less "polished" than others—I was forced to start to examine my own critical practice and skills. I was haunted by the question of what to do with texts that did not conform to the aesthetics that I had been taught to appreciate. Moreover, I continued to approach such texts as mere bridges to move students from one set of reading tastes to one that is considered to be more refined and therefore inherently more valuable. However, the more time I spent thinking critically about popular fiction, the more I became convinced that such work has a value of its own, which exceeds its function to bring the lay readers tastes into harmony with academic tastes.

For example, in his work assessing the impact of canons on the study of American Literature, *Canons and Contexts*, Paul Lauter emphasizes the idea of student engagement as a standard of merit. Though Lauter is not concerned with popular literature in particular, his concern with the affective potential of noncanonical texts makes his observations quite relevant for thinking about popular fiction since the potential for identification or being "relatable" is such a definitive factor in successful popular fiction. One important suggestion he makes is that student audiences are less concerned with the kinds of formalist analysis that engages the professoriate. Rather, "the core for most of our students remains the experiences they encounter in the books and poems we bring them to."[1] Moreover, Lauter reminds his readers that "our views of literary excellence derive largely from criticism of recent vintage" which developed, largely, to justify the expertise of the professional literary critic.[2]

The effect, of course, of the literary critics' training in formal analysis is that she will most often choose texts that support such approaches. Like Lauter, though, I believe that engaging textual affect is as valuable as conducting formalist analysis. Thus, bringing into the classroom and our scholarship some texts, which may not seem to meet the "literary" aesthetic, but which are emotionally compelling and present unique opportunities to develop a richer understanding of a given period or theme in the literature. Although they are few, calls for an examination of popular African American fiction do tend to this perception by emphasizing how this literature can help us to more fully understand the complex and varied experiences of the post–civil rights era.[3] In addition to providing a better understanding of significant social attitudes and experiences of the post–civil rights era, another possible result of bringing the formalistic and affective approaches together is the reinvigoration of African American literature as part of the public sphere.

Given my interest in explicating the political potential of popular African American literature, I decline to engage the question of aesthetic standards or merit to any significant degree. Instead, I assume that the merit of teaching and analyzing various forms of popular literature resides in its functional consistency with the African American literary tradition. My use of the term popular denotes concern with immediate socio-historical circumstance and thematic resonance over formal sophistication. These characteristics are, in my estimation, as important to the designation "popular" as sales or critical perception, which are more common ways of marking a distinction between the popular and the literary. Focusing on popular literature's concern with lived reality and the affective potential of telling such stories, reveals that

African American popular literature constitutes an important aspect of the black public sphere by addressing questions that are of wide-ranging significance to majorities of black people in a given historical moment.

Black women's popular writing provides a particularly salient example of these historical and affective dynamics. Over and above the fact that women tend to be dominant in the production of African American literature, there are several distinctive ways that their work makes important contributions to black public discourse. First, they foreground gender in ways that are frequently missing from other modes of discourse on contemporary black experience. Second, they exhibit a responsiveness and timeliness to the shifting terrain which is reflected in the rapidly shifting styles and themes which characterize popular fiction. Finally, they continue the historical engagement of the black body as a symbol of political meaning in the social context of the United States.

Although other forms of African American narrative that can also be understood to engage dimensions of black publicity have emerged in the post–civil rights context, they have tended not to engage black female experience as a significant aspect of black identity. Here I am thinking specifically of the highly contrasting modes of narrative associated with post-soul literature and hip hop musical production. Indeed, each of these movements has registered and resisted important aspects of the exclusionary politics of the post–civil rights era. Hip hop musical culture has offered salient challenges to the ongoing practice of race-based economic exclusions, and the post-soul artist has exposed the exclusionary effects of media construction of black culture as homogenous other even as they have been primarily concerned with representations of black masculinity. In fact, they have produced such compelling representations of black male experience in the post–civil rights era that each has achieved a level of authority that has the effect of diminishing our perception of the multiplicity of black identity.[4] Each of these aesthetic movements has been the subject of extensive scholarly attention (although discussion of the hip hop aesthetic tends to reflect cultural studies perspectives rather than literary methods), which has the effect of validating them as forms of cultural production and ensuring that there is a public engagement of those issues and experiences captured in these movements. By contrast, the relative lack of scholarly attention that has been paid to black women's popular writing, from any disciplinary perspective, perpetuates an unconscious high culture/low culture divide. The danger of perpetuating such a schism is that we miss opportunities for the kinds of dialogic interactions that animate the ideal public sphere in which people "gather and share information, debate opinions, and tease out their political interests and social needs with other participants."[5]

The post-soul aesthetic, for instance, has attempted to carve out new ways of engaging a black literary tradition by raising questions about the relevance of civil rights ideology to contemporary experiences of blackness, by articulating the relation of African American culture and American culture broadly construed, and by utilizing alternative narrative forms. Ironically, the more institutionally acceptable post-soul literature operates along a similar trajectory as much popular fiction in its departure from canonical tradition. For instance, its heavy reliance on parody and pastiche of popular culture depictions are out of step with the themes and form that are considered to be the hallmark characteristics of African American literature. The notion of the individual as presented from a post-soul perspective challenges the traditional notion of the African American subject as a singular representative of an undifferentiated group experience. Additionally, post-soul narrative reliance on popular culture references complicates and sometimes subverts the primacy of a folk tradition based in African orality. Such shifts away from these approaches have led many to question how and if such literature can possibly accomplish what has been understood to be the ultimate purpose of African American literature—black political advocacy. The post-soul aesthetic does not give up on political advocacy as much as it reorients that advocacy toward a distinctive generational experience that is concerned with the positioning of black people as individuals in the here and now rather than the position of the collective historically. Many see this as a kind of cultural amnesia. Nonetheless, I see a benefit to the forced disaggregation of black communal concerns. It forces us to be critical about the bases of our collective identity. Consequently, the value of such literary heresy is its intervention in the public articulation of black identity.

However, the critical attention to difference that the post-soul aesthetic was supposed to enable was quickly undermined by its adoption within academe and public intellectualism. Such institutionalized positions, of necessity, reflect their positioning as sites of power. It comes as no surprise then, that what was, early on, imagined as a way of describing how African Americans spoke from multiple class, aesthetic, and ideological positions, soon lost track of varied class positions and was utilized in a way that focused on the black middle class in an oppositional relationship with working-class aesthetics.

As hip hop based representations of blackness became more commercially and critically prominent, applications of post-soul theorizing became more focused on those representations which challenged working-class representations of blackness and tried to clear space for middle-class black experience as an equally valid and "real" representation of black identity. Moreover, even when the post-soul perspective actively "instigated an aggressive, oppositional criticism that embodied the sonic kinetics of hip-hop" it did so in a way that was "primarily defined by black male sensibilities."[6] Thus, the very valuable potential of a critical and artistic perspective intended to examine blackness from its own margins was crippled by its failure to recognize femininity as one of blackness's interstitial spaces.

In contrast, African American women writers across popular genres have demonstrated the affective potential of literature to articulate "shared experiences" that "can bond people together in ways that far exceed language."[7] The opposition of language and feeling proposed is an interesting one that returns us to the troublesome question of aesthetics. Academic practice has tended to fetishize language and to approach literature in a way that, as Paul Lauter describes, dissociates "what a work is about and how it affects us from the ways in which it is put together."[8] One result of this dissociation is the difficulty I describe above of knowing how to deal with a text that does not meet our expectations in terms of sophistication in language and structure.

Some critics have recently begun to address such issues in relation to contemporary urban fiction.[9] Variously they argue that we can approach such texts by reading them through theories of spectacle or by paying close attention to the act of writing as an assertion of agency. In both cases, the implication of their approaches is that we re-center the affective dimension of a text in our analyses. In turn, I am suggesting that popular literature's affective potential and the bonds it can create are of particular importance to the cultivation of a black public sphere in a time when, by many accounts, fragmentation among African Americans is one of the most crucial obstacles to a black counter-public.[10] Thus, I forgo any extended discussion which would attempt to justify the inclusion of popular literature in critical practice on the basis of aesthetic merit. Instead I focus on the ways in which popular writing by African American women serves to create a dialogic account of female gender experiences as they intersect with class differentiation within the African American community, with shifts in generational experience, and with the public policy landscape. In focusing my attention on these popular forms, I am inspired by Mae Gwen Henderson's notion of dialogism.

The dialogic nature of black women's writing, as specified by Henderson in her 1989 essay, "Speaking in Tongues" is as much in evidence today as it was in the period in which she initially explicated it. Black women's writing, including the popular, speaks to and from the various social and aesthetic positions which have emerged in the post–civil rights era, enabling a critical project which makes legible the common goals and values of multiple discursive communities. It is my intention here to show how the "dialogic of difference and dialectic of identity" which Henderson finds at work in early twentieth-century African American women's texts can help to situate and advance critical engagement with the popular literature of the present era.[11] The dialogic of difference, which names the contestatory nature of black women's writing, is located in part in the popular writers' bold choice to speak from the literary margins. However, to speak from the margins does not mean to wholly adopt the position of an outsider and in their extension of key aspects of the African American literary tradition, writers of popular fiction enact the dialectic of identity, which emphasizes aspects of shared experience and collective narrative enterprise. Thus, examining the multiple positions from which black women writers speak illuminates the diversity of experience which constitutes contemporary black life. The result of such "simultaneous discourse" is a resolution to the problem of competing aesthetic discourses described above and makes an important contribution to the larger public discourse on contemporary black identity.

The significance of speaking from the literary margins can be measured by the extent to which the recent crisis over the fate of African American literature has been motivated by the commercial dominance of popular fiction.[12] The ascendance of Buppie fiction in the 1980s and early 1990s first, and the subsequent rise of street lit/urban fiction and black erotica, has led to an animated discussion which sometimes posits the end of African American literature as we know it. These popular forms are seen to be out of line with the aesthetic and political standards established in the context of the academic institutionalization of African American literature in the latter part of the twentieth century. The substance of the critique regarding such literature has been two-fold, denigrating both the perceived lack of aesthetic quality and the failure to represent an activist politic.

In failing to centralize race in ways that are consistent with the Reconstructionist canon, popular literature has come to be associated with the potential death of African American literature rather than an indication of its evolution. A central question, posed repeatedly in interviews with authors, on discussion boards, and in professional editorials is what is the relationship between black popular fiction (genres such as romance, street lit, erotica, and Christian fiction, for example) and traditional, or "real" black literature. Implicit in this question is the assumption that the relationship is, in point of fact, a zero-sum relationship in which the vitality of one is figured as a death-knell for the other. However, I propose that in continuing to privilege those texts which are most obviously linked to the "traditional" canon, we miss important opportunities to widen the scope of our understanding beyond the dichotomies of post-black/old black, which force us into a fallacious debate over the viability of African American literature as a distinctive entity. In privileging narrative strategies that reinforce their relationship with a mass audience and its concerns, the voices of popular women writers challenge the marginalization of black women in the public discourse on black identity. Because the arena of popular literature is dominated by women as readers and writers, attending to this work would necessarily help us to recalibrate broadly defined racial concerns to account for the specific ways that gender informs those concerns.

Moreover, the emphasis on the question of what the rise of popular literature means for the fate of African American literature as we have defined it
obscures the equally salient question of what constitutes *public* discourse.
Even the latest model with which we have been working, which frames
media as the most significant manifestation of black publicity, has not fully
accounted for the degree to which even the discourses within it are shaped
via the "blogosphere" and "twitterverse" by a professional intellectual class
whose interpretations may or may not function to bind communities together.
Turning to the relationship of black popular writers to their audiences, however, allows us to locate an aspect of black public discourse in which the
values and concerns of multiple demographics carry significant weight in the
expressions that, presumably, represent them. Thus, I centralize the affective
dimension of the texts examined by focusing on these texts' strategies for
offering realistic depictions of familiar experiences which invite identification on the part of the audience.

Within this body of literature there is a characteristic of social reflexivity
that opposes the trans-historical orientation of the novelistic tradition which
emerged after the 1970s. The emergence of this trans-historical approach
marked a consequential new development in the tradition of African
American letters. It simultaneously contributed to more rigid distinctions of
high and low forms and, to some extent, placed black literary production at a
removal from the black public sphere. Popular culture material is necessarily
concerned with the lived experience of contemporaneous audiences, who, of
course are situated historically, but are unlikely to frame their daily experiences in historical terms. High cultural forms, on the other hand, tend to be
conceived of as engaging more enduring and abstract components of human
experience and to reify the separation of the everyday, mundane aspects of
human experience from those which transcend the ordinary. Thus, the development of this thematic concern with history in African American literature
contributes to a unique development in which African American writing is
less likely to be simultaneously "literary" and "popular" at the same time. [13]

As a significant but critically neglected part of the new media ascendance,
the production of black women writers complicates extant analyses of racial
representation by focusing attention on issues of class and gender in the
academy, in the collective social lives of African Americans, and in the arena
of national policy, making a crucial intervention in the black public sphere.
Through my examination of black women's popular literature in this book, I
demonstrate how this literature can engender challenges to the ways that we
consider the authority of the critic and critical reading practices as well as the
ways in which popular writers are alternatively authorized through their relationships with audiences and their engagement of black identity politics
through thematic rather than formal approaches.

Key among these themes is what the black woman's experience is in the here and now. We find in the contemporary literature black women speaking from highly specified social locales, which reveal the ways in which black female experience is nuanced by class positioning, the availability of new categories of identity, and the spatial politics of integration. Deeper critical engagement with such texts, then, is critical to understanding African American literature as it indexes African American experience, for as Herman Beavers proposes in his essay, "African American Women Writers and Popular Fiction," the response of audiences to this work has less to do with "their explication of African American female experience on a historical grid" than with "their depiction of African American women's experiences in the post–civil rights era."[14]

Even the forty or so years that we call the post–civil rights era reflects some distinctive social contexts that impact the nature of black women's social and political experiences. As a result, my analyses are similarly historicized, examining representative texts from three distinct social periods—the immediate post–civil rights era, the Affirmative Action period, and the Neoliberal era. I settle on these periods because they help us to understand the ways in which black women's literature has been in dialogue with the black and American public culture.

From the 1970s to the present, we have witnessed a number of media innovations that have presented black women as symbols which were indicative of the social conception of black people as a whole. In the 1970s we witnessed the emergence of the "liberated" black woman in film and television media. From television's Christy Love, to Motown's biopic representation of the tragic life of Billie Holiday, *Lady Sings the Blues*, black women were entering into the panorama of American visual representation in a wider variety of roles than ever previously witnessed. Although such images did signify in ways that were specifically gendered, the choices that these female characters faced were also meta-commentaries on newly liberated black subjects. The choices that fictional black women characters made regarding their relationships to larger structures of power—like the law or corporate enterprise—paralleled the dilemma of the black community as a whole in its effort to assess the nature of its new relationship to a state which had presumably opened its arms to its black citizens. Moreover, there was a general consistency in the celebratory ways in which black femininity was framed, whether it came from mainstream or independent black media sources. By the 1990s media representations had shifted and there was less consonance between black produced images and those which dominated "mainstream" media outlets. In fact, black self-representation had departed significantly from the majority point of view. Black-generated imagery was focused on representing the unconflicted success of black professional women, while news media were largely focused on the black woman as social menace, through the image of the welfare queen. By the beginning of the new millennium, the success of hip hop culture had once again shifted the image of the black woman in media representations. Through the rise of music video culture the black woman had become a symbol of wanton sexuality or merely a victim of black male misogyny.

In each of these periods, even as representations of black women have been central to the discursive construction of African American relations to the nation, at no point have actual black women been a significant presence in the institutions framing the discourses. We cannot identify any black women directors, producers, or script writers who could be seen to frame the image of the black woman in the 1970s. In the 1990s there were a number of black women holding political office by election or appointment but few who were positioned to shape the discourse on affirmative action or welfare re-form from proactive position rather than a defensive one. Nor have African American women been especially well-positioned to shape the conversation on the nature of black culture to which critiques of hip hop culture are often linked. As a consequence, in the context of non-literary or non-fictional media forms, black women's voices have been relatively excluded from the public sphere.[15]

On the other hand, within the context of literary production, African American women have gained more authority than ever before. Their inter-nalization of this authority can be illustrated through a consideration of one of the major archetypes of black women's fiction—the conjure woman. The conjure woman has been the subject of much scholarly attention as a figure that offered an image of empowerment along lines of race/culture and gender simultaneously. The title and introduction to Marjorie Pryse and Hortense Spillers's 1985 collection, *Conjuring: Black Women, Fiction and Literary Tradition*, gives some sense of the resonance of the conjure figure. The collection begins with a discussion of a closing note in Alice Walker's novel, *The Color Purple*, in which Walker thanks her characters for coming to her. Pryse's explication frames Walker as a kind of conjurer herself, to the extent that she becomes the medium through which the character Celie, "who lacks a formal education and who writes her letter (and the novel) in the colloquial English of southern, black, poor, and barely literate country people" is able to take form.[16] The relationship between Walker and her character is a mutua-listic relationship which echoes the ethos of Black Arts Movement communi-tarianism as well as the black feminist project of tradition building as Pryse characterizes it: "Walker seems to be saying that Celie's ability to write her story is a precondition for her own ability as a novelist."[17] By contrast, the success of black women writers from Walker and Morrison to McMillan and Stringer, means that the twenty-first century offers few obstacles to a black woman imagining herself as a novelist. Thus the tropes which capture the imagination of contemporary writers tend to be oriented in other directions—

she is neither conjuring a new role for the black woman, nor breaking ground from which the dispossessed speak.

Instead, in contemporary African American popular literature, the black woman has been placed, unselfconsciously, at the center of black women's writing. The feeling of legitimacy that is engendered by the success of black literary and popular fiction becomes the basis for new approaches. What makes the work of popular women writers unique is the highly specific nature of their representations. The tendency within this genre of work is not to treat women as a generalized other. Instead, what I find is that each historical moment produces an engagement of black female experience in a relation to a specific set of discursive conditions. They represent experiences that respond to generalized media representations of black women, to black communal constructions of black femininity as well as to codes of behavior that emerge specifically from within black female culture. This is accomplished through challenges to existing black female archetypes and through the generation of new archetypes.

Those which I examine include the cultural mulatto, the Buppie, the Bitch, the Diva, and the Baby Mama. Each of these archetypal figures negotiates a particular set of socio-historical formations as well as particular iconic formulations of black femininity. The cultural mulatto is associated with the disruption of Black Nationalist ideology. In particular, I associate it with the disruption of the reactionary politics of gender that inhere in nationalist thought. The Buppie figure of Girlfriend fiction asserts the legitimacy of economic aspiration in the face of the assault on black progress that was the anti-affirmative action movement of the turn of the millennium. The Bitch, Diva, and Baby Mama are products of the deviant constructions of black femininity that converge in neoliberal political discourse and hip hop culture's hypersexual narrative content. Through such characters contemporary black women writers offer insights into the forms the black female quest for social power takes in the post–civil rights era. The sheer number and variety of black women writers and readers itself represents a change in black women's self-perception in both social and symbolic forms.

In the first chapter, I survey the politics of canon formation in the early post–civil rights era, linking it to the development of a set of critical reading practices which continue to inform how we as scholars approach a rapidly evolving body of literature. In it I describe how a particular notion of the vernacular comes to dominate the academic conception of African American literature to the exclusion of the real-life reading practices of black consumers and producers of literature. These developments are part and parcel of a shift in the institutional contexts for the production of scholarship on the subject of African American literature. Indeed, as literary authority moved from independent black institutions into the halls of the academy, even more factors arose to contribute to the separation of popular and literary forms.

The very nature of academic production is at odds with the dynamics of popular writing. This is the case not only in aesthetic terms but with regard to the temporal processes which govern each. Where popular cultural production is concerned with the lived experiences and cultural habits of subjects *in situ*, the processes of academic production are not always as explicitly concerned with the implications of scholarly insights for the day-to-day lives of its subjects. Moreover, the temporal cycles of the academy are so expansive that the scholarship is almost invariably referencing conditions that have already shifted by the time the ideas are in circulation, further distancing it from lived conditions.

In chapters two and three I focus on a set of texts which challenge the authority of professional critic. First, I offer a case study of critical practice around Toni Morrison's *Tar Baby*, demonstrating how the reading from a traditional historical perspective produced a fairly singular but incomplete reading of its textual dynamics. Foregrounding the novel's engagement of the complex intersection of race, gender, and social context, I read the protagonist from multiple angles. Situating her in the context of patriarchal gender ideologies, social and global changes of the 1970s, and in relation to twenty-first century aesthetics produces a composite of black female experience in the immediate post–civil rights era. As a further challenge to the hegemony of the critic, chapter three examines some of the narrative strategies popular black women writers have employed to acknowledge the authority of black readers in the validation of black literary enterprise. Through readings of Girlfriend fiction, I contrast the impact of audience-based black vernacular style with scholarly deployments of the vernacular. These novels express the socio-reality of black women interrogating the iconic representations of black women in the Affirmative Action era.

Finally, chapters four and five move even further toward the margins of black literary production to examine the fundamental challenges to academic and popular literary authority launched by women of the hip hop generation, who engage contemporary racial formations in economic rather than aesthetic or cultural terms. Focusing on the production of women writers in the "street lit" genre helps to fill a gap in the scholarship. This scholarship has been extremely valuable in suggesting how street lit authors of the 1960s and 1970s—such as Robert Beck (a.k.a. Iceberg Slim), Roland Jefferson, and Odie Hawkins—can be read in ways that complicate some of our current assumptions regarding distinctions between literary aesthetics and reading publics, but it necessarily focuses on the production of black male authors. Examining contemporary "street lit" or urban fiction provides an opportunity to examine how women use the genre. In chapter four, I demonstrate the ways in which black women writers of the hip hop era engage black feminism in a way that reflects their own unique positioning via the social and economic structures of the turn of the twenty-first century. The final chapter positions tell-all memoirs by women of the hip hop generation as an extension of the urban fiction genre and explores how their self-narration encodes resistance to public neoliberal discourses of black femininity.

NOTES

1. Lauter, 102.
2. Ibid., 104.
3. See Herman Beavers's and Dana Williams's essays in *The Cambridge Companion to African American Women's Literature*.
4. In the essay "Postmodernism, Pop Music, and Blues Practice in Nelson George's Post-Soul Culture," David M. Jones offers a provocative discussion of hip hop culture in the post-soul era. He argues that scholarly attention to hip hop culture at the expense of other black musical forms echoes and reinforces popular media's presentation of hip hop culture as representative black culture.
5. Squires, 148.
6. Neal, *Soul Babies*, 110.
7. Joyce A. Joyce, "The Black Canon: Reconstructing Black American Literary Criticism," *New Literary History*, 18, 2 (Winter 1987): 335–344.
8. Lauter. *Canons and Contexts*, 105.
9. I am thinking specifically of essays by Kristina Graaff and Eve Dunbar included in *Contemporary African American Literature: The Living Canon*.
10. For some examples see Eddie Glaude, Jr., *In a Shade of Blue: Pragmatism and the Politics of Black America*, Michael Dawson, *Black Visions: The Roots of Contemporary African American Political Ideologies*, and Catherine R. Squires, "Rethinking the Black Public Sphere: An Alternative Vocabulary for Multiple Public Spheres."
11. Henderson, "Speaking in Tongues," 12.
12. Two separate moments of doomsday prophesying capture critical attention again and again: Thulani Davis, "Don't Worry Be Buppy," and Nick Chiles, "Their Eyes Were Watching Smut." Both are op-eds published in 1994 in the *Village Voice* and 2006 in *The New York Times*, respectively.
13. For a historical overview of this argument see Candice Love Jackson's essay 'From Writer to Reader: Black Popular Fiction' in *The Cambridge History of African American Literature*.
14. Beavers, 272.
15. For some discussion of the reception of black women's voices in political culture, see Melissa Harris-Perry, *Sister Outsider*.
16. Pryse, *Conjuring*, 1.
17. Pryse, 2.

Chapter One

The Reconstructionist Canon, Black Feminist Literary Perspectives, and Popular Potential

At this point, the debate between Joyce Ann Joyce and Henry Louis Gates around the purpose of African American criticism is probably one of the best known historical debates in African American literature. It marked the moment of some significant developments in the institutional life of African American letters. In this book, I suggest that we have arrived at a similar moment in which the confluence of social changes and new trends in publishing require a reexamination of critical and pedagogical practice. This necessity is reflected in recent efforts to account for contemporary writing by African American women, which have reinvigorated debates regarding canons and canon-making.

Instead of drawing lines of distinction between the now cliché "old dead white men" and the literature of the multicultural United States and the post-colonial world, as in the 1980s, the current interrogation is driven by the ascendance of many forms of popular fiction in the twenty-first century marketplace. The exuberant reception of such writing by African American women has led to "An inevitable conversation around this issue of 'pop culture writing as "literature"'[which] has already begun to sound off in the halls of academia, forcing critics to either defend or to expand traditional ideas of canon formation" according to Dana Williams.[1] Because such writing is arguably, a direct consequence of the critical and artistic struggles of African American women in the late twentieth century, thoughtful, nuanced contributions to this conversation are just as necessary now as the space clearing efforts of the 1980s were then.

1

In this chapter, I situate my own entry into to this conversation by examining the contributions and limitation of some of the major critical and aesthetic approaches of the post–civil rights era. I offer some historical context for the current critical practices and perspectives by highlighting black feminist criticism's relationship to the Black Arts Movement, describing the impact of critical practice developed in the Reconstructionist period on general understandings of African American vernacular culture and, finally, by suggesting how these trends have led to the professional crises that mark this particular historical moment. In tracing out a brief history of critical and creative trends, it is not my goal to throw the proverbial baby out with the bath water but to recall the fact that the African American literary project, however it is defined in a given moment, is always one that is historically situated. I begin by examining the relationship between the Black Arts Movement and the rise of black feminist criticism and the limits of the Reconstructionist movement. Then, I discuss the development of post-soul and hip hop aesthetics as reactions to the narrowing of academic approaches to African American literature. Finally, I suggest the ways in which black women's popular writing synthesizes the most ideal characteristics of each of these movements, moving us closer to the political vigor that has been the most significant characteristic of African American literature, historically.

AFRICAN AMERICAN LITERARY AESTHETICS IN THE IMMEDIATE POST–CIVIL RIGHTS ERA

In examining the contours of black feminist critical perspectives since the 1970s we find a rigorous conversation which reflects a dialogic engagement with contemporary issues as well as the past. Collectively, the critical and creative output of black women in the late twentieth century shows the impact of the style and ethos of self-definition realized by Black Arts Movement. However, black feminist criticism did not limit itself to a racialist understanding of how American literature needed to be reconceived. African American women writers and critics took to heart the lessons of the movement and adapted them to their own agenda of creating space for black women within the canon of African American literature. Such space clearing took place largely in the context of the academy. As Farah Jasmine Griffin observes, "by the mid-1990s black feminist literary studies was one of the most intellectually exciting and fruitful developments in American literary criticism."[2] Similarly, critics such as Barbara Christian and Kalamu ya Salaam position black women writers as the successors to the vanguard position previously held by the Black Arts Movement artists.[3] Since their work was a pivotal component of the mainstream institutionalization of African American literature in the academy, understanding the ways in which black women as writers and critics have engaged the aesthetics of African American literature is crucial to understanding the development of the field since the 1970s.

In his innovative study of the Black Arts enterprise, Howard Rambsy describes the means by which the Black Arts Movement shifted the terms of African American literary production. He delineates the ways in which critical authority was wrested from the control of traditional institutions through publication strategies and by the artists' assumption of the role of critic. He notes that in attempting to "establish common objectives and solidify shared interests" writers such as Larry Neal, LeRoi Jones, Carolyn Rodgers, and Sarah Webster Fabio tended to address themselves to their fellow black writers.[4] This latter move which he describes as the poets, critics, and theorists becoming one establishes some important antecedents for contemporary approaches in that it allowed for an approach to the analysis of African American literature which utilized "African American verbal styles as an approach for categorizing the writings."[5] In other words, it laid the foundation for legitimating the presence of vernacular culture in African American literary forms.

In addition to the focus on verbal styles as an important category of analysis, Rambsy also attributes to the Black Arts Movement an aesthetic which privileged black music and musicians as literary influences.[6] This emphasis on music was part of the Black Arts Movement artists' interests in specifying a "pure" black artistic lineage. Music was presumably more useful to this project because, unlike the written tradition up to that point, it was safe from the contamination of Euro-American aesthetic norms. Such an approach not only reified black vernacular culture, it marked a definitive movement away from the usual method of literary periodization. African American musical culture provided themes and formal structures that reflected the concerns of black public culture in that moment. Thus, Black Arts Movement critics reoriented the usual cartography of literary movements by incorporating alternate genealogies. As the writers defined their tradition, they did not recognize the existence of a distinct black written tradition. Consequently, the movement which they wrought was necessarily centered on the work of a living, breathing community of peers.

The importance of a living tradition was no less clearly demonstrated than articulated. For example, an examination of Neal's primary assumption—that the Black Arts Movement was "radically opposed to any concept of the artist that alienates him from his community" and that it was the "spiritual sister" of the radical new politics of the Black Power movement—shows how this assumption is reflected in the way he builds his argument.[7] He simultaneously defines and illustrates the principles of the black art aesthetic by engaging the work of his contemporaries. He traces out the themes and formal characteristics of plays by LeRoi Jones, Ben Caldwell, Ron Milner, and Jimmy Garrett and infers that these are the definitive characteristics of the Black Arts.[8]

The impact of such methods can be seen in anthologies of the era, which skew toward the output of the living writer and a canonical tradition rooted in a contemporaneous perspective.[9] The focus on the present was not merely a rejection of what was perceived as the assimilationist tradition of the Harlem Renaissance and its immediate heirs, though it was, of course, that too. The privileging of contemporary writers was connected to the Black Arts perception of the political work to be accomplished by means of the art. These writers were (re)negotiating the meanings of blackness in the wake of the civil rights movement; a period in which separate black institutions were more a social necessity than a political choice. They symbolized something more than a strategy for social equity, they were expressions of the valorization of black social experience and culture independent of comparisons with Euro-American culture. Thus, those artists who were concerned with articulating where black people were at in that particular moment were seen as central to the living literary tradition. Moreover, the concern with building new black institutions was predicated on the idea of black mass leadership, reflecting the influence of Marxist-based social theories which positioned the proletariat as the vanguard of any revolutionary movement, and centralized forms, styles, and themes which reflected the preferences of that audience.

This investment in an immediate relationship between black writers and readers reflects a set of assumptions that would diminish as African American literature became more deeply institutionalized in the academy. These assumptions included beliefs as simple as the idea that African American literature was a distinctive and coherent body of literature that could be analyzed on its own terms. The relative success of the movement is evidenced by the way that Black Arts Movement artists were able to use the authority they developed by editing their own journals, publishing their own anthologies, and establishing their own analytical criteria, to leverage power in dominant cultural institutions—particularly the academy. The value of such independent institutions for creating black artistic and critical autonomy becomes evident when one begins to examine the shift that occur as Black Arts institutions such as Hoyt Fuller's *Negro World/Black Digest*, Dudley Randall's Broadside Press, or Joe Goncalves's *Journal of Black Poetry* become defunct. As spaces which nurtured Black Arts discourse and perspectives shrank, the power to define what black expression was or should be became more concentrated in the hand of a relatively few academic critics working in predominantly white spaces.

As African American literature was formalized and codified in order to legitimate its presence in the academy, some elements of the Black Arts aesthetic were reified while others were left to wither on the vine in what has come to be referred to as the Reconstructionist movement. In this contentious period, power shifts away from "scholars with black aesthetic approaches" to those whose formalism constitutes a "de facto prohibition against extraliterary concerns in the study of African American literature. . . ."[10] Foremost among the scholars attempting to negotiate this shifting terrain are black feminists. However, their employment of the strategies of the Black Arts Movement in the context of academe yields distinct results.

Within the academy, the prominence of Structuralist and post-Structuralist theoretical approaches, combined with the need to demonstrate an expansive African American literary tradition, re-centered the written tradition that the Black Arts Movement had rejected. This confluence of needs and values produced a catalog of themes and archetypes that were employed to demonstrate the coherence and particularity of African American literary aesthetics. Ironically, black vernacular culture continued to be central to the scholarly engagement of African American literature. However, scholars tended to look to the past rather than the present when identifying those vernacular influences.

Black feminist criticism employed these methods very successfully. Farah Jasmine Griffin sums up their accomplishments:

> In order to construct a tradition that led to contemporary writers such as Morrison and Walker, critics charged themselves with locating, teaching, and writing about earlier "lost" works by African American women. Second, they created a critical vocabulary and framework for discussing works by African American women. Third, they theorized that body of work as well as the critical practices of black feminist critics.[11]

Black feminist critics' efforts to define a tradition closely mirror the tasks associated with the development of the Black Arts Movement; to define a coherent tradition (which evinced a shared origin in vernacular culture), establishing categories of analysis (such as political function or perspective), and developing broad explanatory models (of the artist's relationship to audiences or artistic tradition, for example). However, the attention black women paid to intra-racial ideologies of (hetero)sexism as an aspect of internalized racism is one of the crucial distinctions between black feminist critical practice and Black Arts Movement aesthetics and, perhaps, the basis of its success in the academy as it provided a point of alliance with the work of white feminism.

The interest and support the black feminist critics and texts elicited led to the development of a critical apparatus that provided the academy the most prominent role in the delineation of a black women's literary tradition. This articulation of a distinctive black woman's tradition was a necessary counter to the historical tendency to view black women's writing as "singular and anomalous" and less "racially significant" than writing by and about black men.[12] However, it also set the study of black women writers on a path that would diverge greatly from the politics of the Black Arts Movement which had, in part, empowered it. The blues figures, conjure women, and patterns of speech and narration that came to define the black female tradition were all associated with black geographies and forms that were no longer dominant in the day-to-day lives of readers.

This temporal orientation is of much consequence in terms of canon-making. Where the Black Arts Movement established a living tradition that spoke much directly to the experiences of its era, the canon, tropes, and themes that emerge from the Reconstructionist movement privileged universalist readings and the documentation of a nineteenth-century tradition. Some residual effects of this change are apparent in current critical practice, which minimizes the significance of mass audience sensibilities and attention to the work of living writers engaging the experiences of a living audience.

HIGH AND LOW VERNACULARS

Ultimately, the move away from mass sensibility and the work of contemporaneous authors shifted the implications of the term vernacular from the Black Arts era to the Reconstructionist era. Drawing on Houston Baker's articulation of vernacular theory, Thomas McLaughlin, offers some useful observations regarding vernacular theories. His analysis is concerned with how consumers utilize pop culture texts in "a forceful assertion of rights to cultural space, a refusal to be left out of everyday culture, and a radical claim to read it as the community sees fit."[13] In order to do so, he argues, these consumers must generate independent readings of various cultural phenomena. Such readings, he argues, operate as vernacular theories and are distinguished from academic theory mainly in the language they use and the lack of prestige associated with them. They are similar to academic theory in that each is an interrogation of social systems from a specific locale. McLaughlin's distinctions raise the interesting question of what happens when a particular vernacular becomes the language of the academy.

For instance, Baker's assertion of the value of vernacular theory is framed in the context of academia. His concern is to suggest how reading from a particular cultural perspective could help to legitimate black texts as part of the cultural space of the academy in particular. This dynamic is slightly different from that described by McLaughlin, in which the consumer does not seek to elevate the form but affiliates with it as a symbol of outsider status. These two orientations reflect the varying assumptions of literary and cultural studies. The former approach reflects the positioning of black literary production in relationship to the canonical "American" tradition which has not fully recognized African American literature (or other minority group literatures) as a central component.[14] The fact that African American literature already exists in a low culture relationship to the American canon may help to explain why, in spite of the emergence of a rigorous engagement of non-literary forms of black popular culture—from televisual representations to musical production—there has been little systematic interrogation of the politics of upholding high culture/low culture distinctions in the context of African American literary production. The positioning of African American literature via American literature has made it seem self-evident that such distinctions primarily serve to uphold status quo relations of power. As a consequence, we have largely skipped over an examination of how these distinctions work in the more narrow confines of the African American system of cultural production.

In thinking about how a hierarchy of high and low forms emerges in the context of African American literature, it is useful to examine the processes of distinction described by Lawrence Levine in his influential study of nineteenth-century cultural hierarchy, *Highbrow/Lowbrow*. In this work, Levine illuminates the mechanisms by which Shakespearean drama and opera are transformed from popular entertainments existing alongside minstrel shows, burlesques, and other vaudevillian forms to the symbols of high culture that we know them as today. His description of an initially undifferentiated corpus of texts which spoke to and for a variety of audiences finds rich parallel in the history of African American literary production. Moreover, the processes of distinction that affect the separation into categories of high and low which he describes also operate along similar lines in the context of African American literature. He describes the physical separation of the audience along class lines, the corporatization of theatrical institutions and the fetishization of particular forms of language by critics as central components of the cultivation of cultural distinction. In the context of African American literature we find similar developments with the social separation of classes that emerges in the post–civil rights era, the institutionalization of African American literary studies within the academy, and the focus on particular tropes as markers of "authentic" black literary voice. Such parallels indicate the likelihood that the hierarchy that exists in American culture at large, also exists within the literary culture of African Americans despite its "low" status relative to "American" literature and despite the fact that it has yet to have been examined at length.

The problem with allowing these dynamics to go unexamined in the production of African American literature is that such hierarchies are counter to the animating force of the literature itself which has historically relied on a dialogic of high and low. To fail to attend to the low, then, leads to the conversation which has of late occupied many in the academy. A central question, which surfaces in numerous literary environments, is what is the relationship between black popular fiction (genres such as romance, street lit, erotica, and Christian fiction, for example) and traditional or "real" black literature. Implicit in this question is the assumption that the relationship is, in point of fact, a zero-sum relationship in which the vitality of one is figured as a death-knell for the other.

In defense of the popular, a few have called for the recognition of hip hop's folk-based storytelling and complex deployment of rhyme and meter as literary production.[15] Those invested in a more traditional notion of literature have, nonetheless, debated whether racial protest themes continue to be of value as a defining characteristic of African American literature. Most recently and controversially, in his book *What Was African American Literature?*, Kenneth Warren argues that African American literature, as a distinctive aesthetic and critical practice was a product of the legal and social strictures of Jim Crow segregation. The historical presumption of black cultural inferiority, he suggests, produced the assumption of black literary inferiority, necessitating the development of a set of standards of critical evaluation which privileged the social function of African American literature as explanations of and tools for the dismantling of the iniquitous system of race in the United States over strictly aesthetic evaluations. It is this approach which constitutes the legacy of contemporary critics and writers alike and which produces the inconsistencies and contradictions with which I want to grapple in these pages.

Given that the social context which produced the assumption that writers of African descent produced a body of literature that was, presumably, both coherent in itself and distinct from other literatures, to a large degree no longer exists, Warren's examination raises an important question regarding how to understand the literary output of contemporary African Americans. He inquires to what extent "those representational and rhetorical strategies that at their peak served to enable authors and critics to disclose various 'truths' about their society can begin to atrophy and become conventionalized so that they no longer enable literary texts to come to terms with social change but operate as practices of evasion."[16] In raising the question of whether we continue to require such a category as African American literature one is raising a question of black publicity as much as anything else.

AESTHETIC CHALLENGES AND BLACK PUBLIC SPHERES

Before the advent of black access to multiple media streams, written literature was one of the main sources of a shared public discourse among African Americans. This important political function of African American literature accounts, in large part, for the historical tendency toward reading, writing, and teaching practices that drew from texts, language practices, and themes which demonstrated a range of cultural positions. African American writers from Frederick Douglass and Harriet Jacobs to James Baldwin and Lorraine

Hansberry incorporated vernacular practices and perspectives into their artistic production with the express purpose of suggesting a collective perception of black experience in the national context. As the black public sphere has become more diffuse—and the author a less authoritative figure—our institutional reading and writing practices have become more fragmented. For instance, scholars of African American literature rarely engage popular literature as literature, some of the most critically lauded African American novelists are virtually unheard of outside academia and many of our most important discussions of race are communicated in 140 characters or fewer. One result of this fragmentation is that there is a tendency for participants in conversations on black public experience to speak from specific social locations.

The emergence of new aesthetic approaches at the dawn of the twenty-first century speaks to these tensions. The post-soul aesthetic, for instance, has attempted to carve out new ways of engaging a black literary tradition by raising questions about the relevance of civil rights ideology to contemporary experiences of blackness, by articulating the relation of African American culture and American culture broadly construed, and by utilizing alternative narrative forms. In the arena of hip hop narrative (both musical and literary) we see the assertion of numerous critiques of the legal and economic experiences of the black disenfranchised. Instead of reading these narratives as a reaction to the narrow field of canonical African American literature, most critical approaches to hip hop culture have been framed in terms of the cultural studies paradigm, foregrounding hip hop's working-class politics and aesthetics. Rarely is hip hop regarded as an extension of black popular literature even though many acknowledge its indebtedness to the urban fiction of the 1970s. Critical reaction to these two very different methods of challenge illustrates the migration of meaning associated with black vernacular theory.

On the one hand, hip hop aesthetics can be associated with notion of the vernacular carved out by Black Arts Movement theorists—that which reflects a mass consciousness. On the other hand, its very dynamism and of-the-moment discursive quality disqualify it from the academic notion of vernacular culture which is more concerned with stable and timeless expressions of black cultural experience. Consequently, hip hop narrative has not been taken seriously as part of the African American literary tradition. However, because it elicits strong affective responses from audiences, its consumption is frequently critiqued as escapist fantasy, and it is often perceived as engaging socially degraded themes, I see the hip hop aesthetic as one which is relevant to a variety of popular forms. Thus, I am associating the hip hop aesthetic with multiple genres of black popular fiction whether or not they reference hip hop culture directly. In doing so, I focus the renegade approaches made possible by the looser terms of production that govern black popular output.[17] Additionally, I interpret certain affective responses among audiences as support for popular literature's vernacular orientation.

Popular literature moves units even when more "elevated" forms of literature do not. More to the point, popular literature generally does so mostly by reflecting and meeting aesthetic values of its particular audience. In the case of African American literature this tendency can be even more pronounced because frequently audiences' identification with the content of the literature is augmented by a sense of identification with the authors who produce this literature. The fact that many of them lack formal training in the arts, frame their literary endeavors in solely economic terms, and self-publish can serve to enhance that sense of identification. For example, authors such as Carl Weber and Kimberla Lawson Roby elicit support as much for their own commitment to black entrepreneurship as for the melodramatic plots of aspiration and betrayal that they produce.

The author talks I witnessed at the 2011 meeting of the National Book Club Conference, a meeting organized by Curtis Bunn to bring together "black book" fans and authors, illustrated this phenomenon. In one session, Weber and Lawson appeared together before a packed room of book club members and other conference participants. Lawson read briefly from her novel in progress, but the bulk of her time was spent describing how she came to writing as an alternative to continuing to bang her head against the glass ceiling of corporate America. Weber, too, framed his discussion in terms of his own personal quest for economic mobility and offered copious and repeated thanks to the audience for supporting his efforts to reach sales benchmarks to which his larger and larger advances were tied. These sessions were remarkable for the level of enthusiastic support and testimonial they elicited. Though both authors' works centralize important facets of contemporary black life such as the continuing role of the church in the organization of black social life and the complex relations of family life, these topics were only one part of the discussion. In addition to their biographies and thematic interests, a third topic of discussion, focused on marketing issues and the placement of "black books" in major retail outlets, further illustrated the complex mechanisms of audience identification.

Many of the attendees expressed dismay at recent moves by retailers to eliminate the African American interest sections and integrate "black books" into the general fiction section. This attitude is in direct contrast to the view commonly held by more conventionally "literary" authors that such interest sections have the effect of minimizing the universal perspectives of their work and narrowing their audiences. As the complaint is framed in terms of creating an obstacle to easily locating titles in which the audience has a specific and singular interest, it reflects a reading dynamic identified by Mary Rogers in her study, *Novels, Novelists, and Readers*, as the habits of the "specialist" reader. This kind of reader "favors formulaic and best-selling novels as well as those portraying subcultures they identify with."[18] More-over this kind of reader is more interested in affirmation than challenge; approaching a novel with a willingness to "follow a fairly unambiguous lead, largely accept narrators' words at face value, experience the types of selves they already know, and enjoy a story."[19] I find this formulation useful for thinking about the affective impact of African American popular literature. In fact, it prompts me to consider just the nature of the experience that consumers of popular African American literature seek.

The emphasis on class tensions, interpersonal drama, and pervasive refer-ences to contemporary popular culture in this body of literature reflect the concerns of everyday people, as Sly Stone would put it. In that way the notion of vernacular culture that plays out in black popular literature hews closely to Black Arts Movement concept of the vernacular, in which work-ing-class, urban experience was central to the language, theme, and style employed. Consumers of urban fiction appear to be interested in a similar address of their particular experiences and authors have recognized that inter-est. This link between black working-class aesthetics and commercial viabil-ity registers the unique class politics of the post–civil rights era. In his essay, "Black Empires, White Desires: The Spatial Politics of Identity in the Age of Hip Hop" Davarian Baldwin argues that the rise of gangsta rap in the mid-1990s ushers in a new discursive construction of blackness in which work-ing-class urban aesthetics—ghetto fabulousness—are uniquely married to material success. This development is remarkable because it eschews the assimilationist stance that has traditionally marked black economic mobility. In their preference for written material that reflects this same ethos, popular audiences can be seen to affirm the recalibration of black identification that takes place in hip hop culture in the late twentieth century.

In contrast to hip hop culture's rejection of assimilationist politics, the post-soul aesthetic has launched a challenge to the very grounds that validate the assumption of the concept of assimilationism. While the goal of each of these aesthetic movements is to advance a conversation on black political identity, the post-soul aesthetic appears, in the main, to address a highly specific post–civil rights experience. While Mark Anthony Neal initially articulated a notion of the post-soul aesthetic that centralized working-class black identity and hip hop cultural production, other delineators of the post-soul aesthetic have theorized a set of concerns in which hip hop culture is often tangential and sometimes even antithetical to the post-soul artistic vi-sion. Neal himself gestures toward his unique take on the post-soul aesthetic in *Soul Babies* when he notes that because of its interest in "negotiating his own [middle] class sensibilities," the ur-text of the post-soul aesthetic, Trey Ellis's 1989 essay "New Black Aesthetic," fails to "mention the ways that hip-hop artists, for instance, also borrow across race and class."[20] Subsequent articulations of this aesthetic, particularly those focused on literary production, highlight the artists' sense of indebtedness to the Black Arts Movement, the critique of civil rights and black nationalist era leaders and discourse, and the self-conscious appropriation of stereotypically white cultural forms, over the influences of hip hop cultural aesthetics. [21]

The framing of these concerns highlights the post-soul self-conception as artists and intellectuals foremost and members of a race, secondarily. In his essay, "Post Black, Old Black," Paul C. Taylor draws attention to the specificity of black artistic concerns by assessing the degree to which Thelma Golden's concept of post-blackness—an art institutional iteration of the post-soul aesthetic—has "transinstitutional" applicability. In doing so, he names artistic production as an institutional site, in which specific problems, such as the constraints engendered by the black vernacular tradition and the difficulty of attaining unracialized access to exhibition spaces, are addressed by the post-black aesthetic. Outside of such institutions, however, he notes that most black people, even of the middle class, do not frame their efforts to expand the meanings of blackness in terms of a break with prior articulations of it. This distinction between institutional and popular attitudes is important because it forces us to examine some of the messier aspects of post–civil rights black discourse; namely, the degree to which institutional voices have come to occupy a hegemonic position in the debate on black identity.

Taylor addresses this in his response to the frequently raised critical challenge to the notion of a post-soul aesthetic—"what in the world is new about black social or artistic diversity?" The answer proffered each time is the temporal location. In his own response to the question, Taylor points to the effects of media representations, while Bertram Ashe directs us to the "freedom" of the post–civil rights era. In addition to the increased physical freedom of the post–civil rights era, the ascendance of black popular culture as well as the increased presence of African Americans in popular culture, generally, has afforded the freedom to experience commercial and social success without strictly imitating the artistic values, speech norms, or social patterns of either the black middle-class or Euro-American culture.

Because of shifts in the black public sphere, however, the implications of such freedom are significant. The emergence of the audience and mass sensibility as significant factors in African American expressive production has reversed, or at least effectively challenged, black institutional authority. Consequently, those contentions which have always raged within the private sphere regarding black communal behavior, perception, and production have spilled over into the public sphere. The immense proliferation of popular media technologies in the late twentieth century and the consequent expansion of vehicles for representing blackness meant that for the first time multiple representations and, more importantly, multiple representatives of black identity played a role in shaping the public discourse on African American desire and aspiration. Voting with their dollars, popular audiences endorse one or another mode of African American expression and wield a level of influence on the production context approaching that of the literary professional of old. However, consumer authority and intellectual authority continue to carry different institutional weight, resulting in the need for further critical examination of the impact of continuing along the same well-worn paths of inquiry to address the question of black identity now. Thus, at the heart of this book's insistence on calling attention to a high/low cultural divide is the desire to help cultivate authority in multiple spaces.

The purpose of describing the class politics of the hip hop aesthetic or the post-soul aesthetic is not to suggest that one is more true or authentic than the other. Each, I would argue, has value in specifying aspects of particular contemporary African American experiences. However, I offer these discussions to draw attention to the limits of such class-bound challenges for fostering a dialogic discourse in African American literature. The deepening gulf between literary and popular themes, styles, and audiences diminishes African American literature's potential to function as a forum "for political redress in the light of the perceived effects of actions that extend beyond those immediately involved."[22]

THE DIALOGIC POSSIBILITIES OF
POPULAR WOMEN'S LITERATURE

In turning to the work of African American women writing in a popular vein, I focus on the way it complicates some of the singular constructions of African American identity I have described above. Its dialogism helps to cultivate a space of black publicity at time when "the tremendous transformations within African American communities and American society . . . have so complicated and intensified contemporary racial politics in the United States that a national black public cannot currently identify and distinguish itself."[23] Since my concern is with how to recreate a dialogic relationship between "high" and "low" literary forms, I focus on the literary production of African American women, who have been at the center of contemporary popular literature since the end of the last century.

As discussed earlier, black feminist criticism has a long and deep commitment to pluralistic politics which has sometimes been over-determined by the political realities of the academy. Reanimating those democratic impulses out of which black feminist criticism grew requires that we connect the canonical tradition with what Lovalerie King calls the living tradition. The living tradition refers not only to the attention we pay to the work of living writers it also entails examining the relationship between writers and readers. In this regard, we can benefit from the insights of several publications which demonstrate the ways in which Reconstructionist notions of the vernacular have obscured some of the complexities of African American literary production, historically.

The work of Maryemma Graham, Elizabeth McHenry, and Harryette Mullen all contributes to our understanding of the losses sustained in the process of literary Reconstruction. They discuss a variety of literatures and literacies that were excised when, in an effort to legitimate African American literature and its study in institutional contexts, critics began to focus on orality and folk aesthetics as hallmarks of African American literary particularity.

In her 1996 article, "African Signs and Spirit Writing," Harryette Mullen troubles critical insistence on the "speakerly" text by pointing out the debilitating dichotomy such an insistence produces: "Presumably, for the African American writer, there is no alternative to production of this 'authentic black voice' but silence, invisibility, or self-effacement."[24] Mullen points the way out of this dichotomy by asking the reader to expand his/her definition of literacy to include visual texts and graphic systems not associated with communication between humans, but between human and divine, and are, thus, illegible to all but those trained in it. The value of such inquiry, Mullen, posits is not only to help us have a more precise understanding of the context of African American literary production, but to similarly enrich our understanding of African American communities and cultures.

By 2002, Mullen's perception is echoed in Elizabeth McHenry's study of nineteenth-century African American book clubs and literary societies. McHenry makes the call that critics dispense "with the idea of a monolithic black community and replace it with a more accurate and historically informed understanding of a complex and differentiated black population."[25] Her contribution to such a project is to put a rich history of producing, consuming, evaluating, and mediating the written word among various African American communities in dialogue with the more common narrative of African American people and African American studies being organized around their "relationship to oral, or vernacular culture."[26] In combination, these critics' insights signpost the way to assessing the impact of such a critical tradition on those currently most likely to produce, consume, or evaluate African American literary production as well as those most likely to be silenced, to be rendered invisible, or to have an effaced presence—women.

Arguably, the most profound effect of the move to establish and legitimate an academic canon of black writing is the elision of the role that black readers' perspectives have historically played in framing black oral and literary discourse. Maryemma Graham offers a compelling account of this history in her essay "Black is Gold: African American Literature, Critical Literacy, and Twenty-First-Century Pedagogies." Therein she argues that the African American scholars moving into the white academy felt pressure to distinguish African American literary enterprise from the working-class values and activist aesthetics of the Black Arts Movement. Establishing "this kind of professional legitimacy" she argues, "required them to distinguish the field itself as much as possible from the social reality that had given rise to it."[27] It also resulted in a decreased value for the literature which captured the imaginations of a non-specialist black reading public and "ensured the development of a certain homogeneity of tastes."[28]

In various ways, each of these critics troubles the common narrative of African American literary particularity, while simultaneously validating a single assumption regarding African American literature: that a significant aspect of its work is to provide a frame of understanding the social experiences of the group. Those experiences are recognized as plural experiences and each critic tries to reorient us to the role of the reader in assuring a literature that reflects that plurality. Though, to a large extent black feminist criticism has been at the forefront of reminding us of such plurality, its unique position as a product of both the Black Arts Movement and the institutionalization of African American literature, means that it has mirrored some of the elements of each.

To the extent that black women's fiction writing of the 1970s challenged traditional notions of race, they are a crucial component of the "freedom" carved out by the Black Power Movement to which the post-soul generation claims indebtedness. However, the degree to which the black feminist literary tradition contributed to the construction of a canon that privileged themes such as "authentic black identity" and communalist values, reified the aesthetics of by-gone eras, and centralized images that emerged from the contexts of slavery and Jim Crow, means that it also helped to necessitate the attempts of post-soul and hip hop aesthetics to challenge the notion of singular black identity, to insist on contemporary formal aesthetics, and to develop its own set of explanatory images and tropes. In her 1994 study *Black Women Novelists and the Nationalist Aesthetic*, Madhu Dubey noted the degree to which "black feminist critics are increasingly turning to metaphors derived from folk culture, such as conjuring, specifying, quilting, and laying on of hands, in order to theorize the distinctive literary and cultural practices of black women."[29]

We must question the value of continuing to privilege a notion of orality rooted solely in the culture of the rural south. In the twenty-first century, when such practices have largely been supplanted by a corporate approach to religious practice, black access to consumer culture and artistic institutions, and the direct speech norms of hip hop culture, to continue to emphasize such tropes above all else is at odds with a critical practice which seeks to illuminate the relationship between black literatures and black ideologies. Moreover, it is a contradictory stance, since those texts which, in the present era, operate in the most speakerly fashion are those which have the least credibility within an academic setting and, consequently, mostly go unexamined. For instance, it is hip hop narrative, both print and musical, which most closely reflects the African American oral tradition and its emphasis on signifying, improvisation, and testimonial, but the print material is eschewed outright, and the scholarly attention to the musical narratives is framed in terms of cultural rather than literary studies. However, if, as Eve Dunbar points out, black women have found a niche from which to represent their own post–civil rights experience in the genre of urban fiction, we miss an opportunity to develop a deeper understanding of the multiple facets of black people's collective experience as well as black women's individual experience.

However useful the elaboration of previous African American cultural formations was for legitimating African American literary scholarship, recent critical enterprise behooves us to assess the degree to which those models are still useful for understanding the literature of the present era. In examining the archetypes presented in the popular fiction of African American women, we are presented with an opportunity to engage a present-day, reader-based black praxis. Such a praxis is not only indicated by the example of the Black Arts Movement but is consistent with a longer history of black cultural self-assessment. W.E.B Du Bois's 1926 essay "Criteria of Negro Art" provides a similar indication of the degree to which an expansion of African American social horizons necessarily entails a reassessment of black identity by means of artistic representation. He describes the social struggles of the African American community: "we have been climbing upward, there has been progress and we can see it day by day looking back along the blood-filled paths. . . . But when gradually the vista widens and you begin to see the world at your feet and the far horizon, then it is time to know more precisely where you are going and what you really want." Moreover, he suggests that this new perspective raises questions regarding the collective identity of African America: "What do we want? What is the thing we are after?"[30]

In my opinion, the characters that people popular fiction can provide answers to Du Bois's questions. For example, characters such as the Bad Bitch and the Diva, which are ubiquitous in popular fiction and memoir, might lead us to conclude that in the twenty-first century, the "Hustle" might be as significant a trope as conjure or the laying of hands was in the nineteenth and twentieth. Just as conjure and laying on of hands functioned to capture the collective sensibility of perceiving power in spaces outside of the dominant culture or a need for healing the spirit of a people, seemingly, forever marginalized, examining the "hustle" as a distinctly African American literary trope carries the potential of capturing something important about black collective experience in the post–civil rights era. It can be a way of simultaneously registering new opportunities as well as the limits which continue to constrain black social and economic advancement. To the extent that "hustle" connotes an aggressive pursuit of one's goal and of excellence, then as a literary trope it could capture the relentless achievement of the black middle class in all fields of contemporary society. At the same time the more common association of "hustle" with a less than legitimate pursuit of economic advancement registers the ways in which many members of the black community continue to be positioned outside more esteemed structures of advancement. Ultimately, though it seems that specifying such a conceptual thread has the potential to articulate classed and gendered experiences simultaneously, diminishing the need to position either as *the* definitive black experience. Rather, such a concept allows us to lay the continuities and distinctions out side-by-side.

NOTES

1. Williams, 81.
2. Griffin, 484.
3. Cited in Rambsy, 156.
4. Rambsy, 133.
5. Rambsy, 134.
6. Rambsy, 145.
7. Neal, 184.
8. Howard Rambsy notes that Carolyn Rodgers employed a similar strategy in her essay "Black Poetry—Where It's At" published in the *Negro Digest/Black World* in 1969. He observes her use of "vernacular terms as headings for her categories [of black poetry], including 'signifying,' 'teaching/rappin,' 'bein,' 'coversoff,' and 'shoutin'" and the strategy of defining them through the use of "examples from New Black Poetry, including excerpts from poems by Amiri Baraka, Sonia Sanchez, Haki Madhubuti, Nikki Giovanni, Ebon, and Barbara Mahone" rather than utilizing the vocabulary of traditional, Eurocentric scholarship.
9. See for example, Michael Harper and Robert Stepto's 1979 collection, *Chant of Saints: A Gathering of Afro-American Literature, Art and Scholarship*, in which living and then newly emerging artists featured most heavily. *Black American Literature: A Critical History*, does not focus solely on living writers but it does explicitly place them in the context of a longer African American literary tradition.
10. Young, 11–13
11. Griffin, 488.
12. Washington, 445.
13. McLaughlin, 66.
14. For an extended discussion of the common conception of the relationship of "minority" and "American" literatures see "Canon Theory and Emergent Practice" in Paul Lauter's *Canons and Context*.
15. See for example, Adam Bradley's *Book of Rhymes* (2009) or Alexs Pate's *In the Heart of the Beat* (2010).
16. Warren, 8–9.
17. See Maryemma Graham "Black is Gold" in *Contemporary African American Literature: The Living Canon*.
18. Rogers, 97.
19. Rogers, 98.
20. Neal, *Soul Babies,* 112.
21. See for example Bertram Ashe's Introduction to the 2007 special issue of *African American Review* devoted to the Post-Soul Aesthetic, "Theorizing the Post-Soul Aesthetic."

22. Here I am drawing on Eddie Glaude's notion of the historical operation of black publics. He articulates this idea in *In a Shade of Blue: Pragmatism and the Politics of Black America*, 144.

23. Glaude, 145.

24. Mullen, 1.

25. McHenry, 14.

26. McHenry, 5.

27. Graham, 8.

28. Ibid., 7.

29. Dubey, *Black Women*, 5.

30. Du Bois, 993.

Chapter Two

Toni Morrison's *Tar Baby* and the Problem of Classification

Toni Morrison's *Tar Baby* offers a unique opportunity to examine the complex interrelationship of high and low art in African American literature. Since it was first published in 1981, as the changes in artistic and scholarly enterprise noted in the previous chapter were solidifying, it is helpful to examine the ways in which this text works in both modes, simultaneously. Morrison's text combines aspects of formal complexity and a thematic engagement of African American history with the gender specificity and temporal orientation of popular approaches. This duality is consistent with African American literary dynamics prior to the Reconstructionist movement. Taking such an approach reveals how neglecting to examine the high culture/low culture divide has impacted the practice of African American scholarship. Because it blurs the lines of popular and literary fiction, the critic can choose which dimensions of the text to emphasize. It has been most consistently read in a literary vein, with critics emphasizing its broad historical dimensions. However, such approaches have produced a rather ambiguous stance toward the text. Contrastingly, reading the text as a proto-popular work opens up space for a more affirmative reading of the central character, Jadine Childs, is a destabilizing factor in many critical readings.

As discussed in the previous chapter, the most common explanation for African American literary distinctiveness is its relationship to the folkloric aspects of African American culture or in terms of its political intention. Such explanations however, do not always serve us well in examining popular literary production. For instance, the tendency with the folkloric approach is to frame folk culture as a product of the past. Rarely do we acknowledge the new forms of lore produced by new social conditions. To the extent that the figures, plot trajectories, and group identification that emerge from

African American folkloric practices are the distillation of a set of experiences which function to memorialize the past in the present, they provide a framework of limited value in understanding a body of literature which examines a set of experiences which are unprecedented in African American history.

Focusing on the political intention of black writing through the framework of post-colonialism has allowed for a more nuanced accounting of the specificities of contemporary experience but nonetheless tends to produce a limited framework for understanding certain kinds of texts. Much post-colonial theorizing posits an antithetical relationship between the white West, associated with the capitalist discourse of progress, industry and civilization, and non-Western people of color, who are symbolically aligned with tradition, nature, and a higher standard of personal ethics. Such a framework produces false dichotomies between past and present, white and non-white cultures, and cultural authenticity and cultural dissolution, obscuring the degree to which the colonial project, especially in the Americas, produced new cultures which were predicated on the synthesis of supposed oppositions.[1]

These two conceptualizations of African American literature—either as a valorization of a distinctive African American culture or as a challenge to white Western ideology—work to support the high/low cultural divide. Each is, in its own way, reflective of the "long view" of history that has characterized the most critically valued work since the 1970s. The intent of such work is primarily to offer an interpretation of history and guide the reader to a given conclusion. On the other hand, popular literature tends to be more concerned with reflecting the forces that shape experience in their own historical moment. The tendency, then, is to take a more open-ended approach that invites reader identification and thus interpretation. One result of this concern with reflection over refraction is that popular literature often embodies multiplicity if not outright contradiction.

These varying historical orientations inform my interest in examining Toni Morrison's *Tar Baby* in relation to popular culture aesthetics and African American critical practice. Morrison's stature as an artist deeply informed by and committed to African American culture, as it has traditionally been defined, is unquestionable. Indeed, for many her work represents the most sophisticated example of the African American literary tradition. Among her extensive body of work, though, *Tar Baby* is distinctive in several ways: it is her only text to include significant white character; it is her only novel that is international in scope; and it is, arguably, her least loved and least taught work. This tension between the perception of this individual text and the perception of her general body of work seems to encapsulate the critical discomfort with African American texts which are not easily explained by appeals to the folkloric or as moralistic critiques of corrupt white structures of power—that is, that do not map along "literary" lines.

The majority of scholarship on *Tar Baby*, which is scant relative to other texts in her oeuvre, has followed one or the other of these traditions and focused on a handful of themes such as Morrison's revision of the tar baby folktale, the presentation of an Africanist world view, and the critique of colonialism that emerges from the novel's rendering of the natural world. All of these perspectives work to keep our attention focused on race as the novel's primary thematic concern since each topic depends on binary notions of white/black culture. However, it is my contention that in order to prioritize race in this way, the scholarship must subordinate the novel's engagement with the complex engagement of gender that destabilizes strictly racialized readings.

Recent scholarship on *Tar Baby* has marked it as a significant transitional moment in Morrison's body of work, has revisited constructions of blackness, and has asked us to think about the relationship between gender and narrative structure. I want to extend such insights and suggest that her work therein constitutes a kind of proto-popular text which anticipates and legitimates the most prominent concerns of African American women writers in the decades following the publication of *Tar Baby*. Major aspects of the plot, some aspects of style, and thematic concerns of this novel share much in common with the "Girlfriend fiction" that will emerge in the late twentieth century. Although the novel interweaves a complex perspective on the black diaspora and the dynamics of colonialism, the plot points are constituted primarily by the story of a romance between a professional black woman and a working-class black man and the obstacles her ambition presents for their relationship.

While none of this means that the novel can be fully characterized as popular fiction, paying attention to those shared characteristics helps me to demonstrate how popular literary forms can help to advance women's participation in the black public sphere through their literary production. Morrison's bilateral approach suggests the importance of black literary perspective that knits together historical and contemporaneous concerns of the black community.

READING THROUGH THE LENS OF GENDER

Examining *Tar Baby* as a thematic forerunner of the popular Girlfriend fiction of the 1990s requires particular attention to the text's positioning of its central character as a female subject. A reading of *Tar Baby* that focuses on Jadine as a gendered and sexed subject exposes the degree to which traditional conceptions of blackness require the omission of such considerations. A central mechanism by which the text draws attention to Jadine as a woman, specifically, is the use of structural parallels between Margaret and Jadine.

The text's emphases on their beauty as a mechanism of social ascent, their subjugation to their male partners and the legacy of suspicion against female sexuality under which they labor expose the way that each is impacted by sexist discourses across racial differences. Such significant parallels compel the reader to examine what common experiences they share along the axis of gender. In this way, the novel puts the interrogation of black female subjection to patriarchal norms on the same plane as its critique of white supremacy.

Margaret Street, the white wife of Valerian Street is almost entirely defined by her looks. She is often referred to as "The Principle Beauty of Maine," and she has attempted to leverage her looks into some form of social mobility and safety through her marriage to the wealthy and powerful candy king, Street. Though her beauty is distinctly white—a notion reinforced by the text's emphasis on her "blue-if-it's-a-boy"[2] eyes and the whiteness of her skin, which she so vigilantly protects—it provides her only limited access to the kind of social recognition she had hoped to enjoy by marrying. While her beauty is enough of a reason for Street to marry her, in other ways it actually limits her autonomy. Her marriage to Street provides freedom from financial cares but reduces her entire being to the role of wife and mother—a role she finds so isolating and constricting that she rebels by enacting physical tortures on "his son" as their cook, Ondine, puts it. Thus, her status as a beauty queen is simultaneously a boon and a trap, based on her embodiment of dominant cultural ideals of white femininity.

Jadine's beauty, too, carries a particular racial resonance. She is the typical "light-skinned beauty" with dark eyes and wavy hair. However, that racialization means something unique in this text and even, as Malin Pereira argues, within Morrison's own body of work: "Unlike the previous three female characters [in Morrison's work prior to *Tar Baby*], who are hurt by, struggle with, and ultimately succumb to internalized [white] views of beauty, . . . Jadine struggles not against white-defined standard of female beauty, but against a black-defined beauty. . . ."[3] Shifting the orientation away from Eurocentrism and toward inter-communal politics reframes the focus from the broad historical view to the particular historical moment that Jadine inhabits. Since her particular kind of somatic "blackness" does not automatically render her unattractive according to the media norms of the day, the reader can more clearly apprehend the way in which Jadine's racially hybrid appearance does render her sexually suspect according to the gender ideology of the culture. Thus, the rendering of her beauty resonates much more closely with a politics of gender and sexuality rather than with the more common critique of beauty hierarchies as an expression of black oppositional politics.

This notion of sexual suspicion leads to an interesting point of comparison between the two characters. The red-haired Margaret is an anomaly within her family of modest-looking people. Her beauty, generally, and her hair, specifically, trouble her father, catching "his eye at the dinner table and ruin[ing] his meals" although "there was no thought of adultery."[4] Morrison's subtle disavowal draws enough attention to the suspicion of his wife's sexual constancy that the reader cannot help but wonder to what extent his wife's piety might be a cover for some less wholesome activity on her part. Because it does not provide any explanation of Margaret's anomalous looks, the narrative leaves the reader to share in the father's residual suspicion even after he remembers the existence of the Buffalo maiden aunts with "hair the color of saffron and the white skin of the north."[5] Moreover, by raising the specter of infidelity, we are reminded of the broad cultural narratives which, across race, construct women as treacherous and lacking restraint.

The notion of female predisposition to deception and heredity are equally salient in the depiction of Jadine, whose very physical appearance, like Margaret, makes her suspect. As one with the appearance of a mixed-race person, Jadine's physiognomy evokes a certain level of suspicion within the novel's black male community, which tends to read her through the historical framework of white male usurpation. In this context, framing her beauty in relation to black self-definition implies not only questions of beauty but also questions of authenticity and cultural loyalty. Such suspicion is exemplified in Gideon's statement regarding Jadine to Son: "Yallas don't come to being black natural-like. They have to choose it and most don't choose it."[6] Describing her as a "Yalla" opposes and diminishes the gold and honey that are the adjectives most commonly associated with Jadine, reducing her to a little valued symbol of white male sexual "appropriation" of black male sexual prerogative and the sense of black female complicity, which subtends the perception of mixed race identity as a particularly feminized form of betraying of blackness. While one might expect that the social changes of the late twentieth century would have rendered such suspicion obsolete, the novel demonstrates in various ways how such attitudes survived into the immediate post–civil rights era. The power of such gendered ideology is not merely reflected in those characters that project this narrative onto Jadine, it is an ideology that she, too, has internalized and must find ways to strategically oppose.

A childhood encounter with a "bitch in heat" is one of Jadine's most formative psychological experiences and one upon which critics rely to explain her character. When she witnesses the female dog's passivity while she is mounted and the way that the female dog bears the brunt of the humans' violent attempts to drive the dogs away, she observes the potential for her own sexuality to make her socially vulnerable and vows to maintain control of her sexuality. This struggle for control is metaphorically rendered in the novel through the image of dogs on silver leashes who tug against Jadine's sexual restraint. However, this image captures more than Jadine's individual struggle to control her own sexual desires. Because this encounter takes place in the streets of Baltimore, where she lived before she became orphaned, it is one that is implicitly linked to her mother and thus comes to signify a kind of female legacy of sexual fallibility.

Her need to be in control of her sexuality stems from her looks, which she has presumably inherited from her mother, and point to the extent to which the mulatta woman has been associated with the betrayal of African American community. Thus, this encounter serves to highlight the intersection of gender and sexuality with Jadine's racial identity. Ultimately, her foundational narrative, provides a contrast to Son's "original dime" story, which symbolizes black male autonomy and his ability to opt out of certain cultural narratives, drawing the reader's attention to the different horizons of possibility for (black) men and women. These divergent gender discourses help to highlight the continuity between Margaret and Jadine as female characters by specifying women's subjection to a pervasive cultural rhetoric of female sexual deviance.

In addition to exposing discursive manifestations of sexism, the novel illustrates some actual strategies of containment which result from the perpetuation of such discourses. Domesticity is a primary strategy of female social containment since it can encompass the contradictory impulses of sexism, the impulse to see women primarily as sexual objects and the desire to regulate their sexuality. Viewed in this light, L'Arbe de la Croix, the Caribbean island-home of Valerian Street, a man typically read as representative of white, Western exploitive values, becomes a site from which we can also read the intersection of masculine privilege across lines of race and class. Within the house for instance, similar metaphors of childish vulnerability are used to elaborate relationships between Margaret and Valerian as well as Jadine and Son. The quarters occupied by Margaret and Jadine are at different times likened to doll's houses. Morrison's use of this doll imagery is telling because it encapsulates notions of female passivity and domesticity as a form of captivity.

In Margaret's case the comparison between her room in L'Arbe de la Croix and her childhood bedroom emphasizes her dependency on Valerian and the lack of qualitative difference between her adult life and her position within her family home. Just as her parents' home had been a space that she misread, so too has she misread the potential of her marriage to Valerian. After she has discovered Son hiding in her closet and Valerian, in turn, invites Son to dinner, Margaret surveys the room and thinks "I have come full circle."[7] Margaret's come full circle to the extent that in spite of having married a wealthy man she has no more social power or personal autonomy than she did as a child seeking the approval of her peers. Just as when she was fourteen and discovered about her trailer home that not everyone thought "the little toilet was cute, or the way the tables folded down and beds became sofas was really neat like having your own dollhouse to live in," Margaret finds once again that her home is a symbol of her place at the bottom of a social hierarchy. Her marriage to Valerian has been as deceptive as the convertible furniture of the trailer since the safety she had expected him to provide (and even the desire to provide it) is belied by his inviting the intruder, Son, to sit down to dinner with them before he asks a single question.

Son attempts to establish a similar dynamic of masculine authority in his relationship with Jadine. After examining the photographs of Jadine which appeared in a fashion magazine and which recount her academic and professional accomplishments, Son's response is to make a comment which reduces Jadine to a sexual object thus exerting a particularly gendered form of control. He asks her how much "dick" she "had to suck" to "get all that gold and be in the movies."[8] Such a response registers Son's desire for Jadine "to be still."[9] That is, he desires that she accept the traditional female role of passive object. As she is presented in the magazine, adorned with the jewels of another unruly female, Catherine the Great, she represents the potential to exert as much force as Son, and he fears "that any moment she might talk back or, worse, press her dreams of gold and cloisonné and honey-colored silk into him . . ."[10] His attempt to contain her takes the form of symbolically stripping her of her blackness when he accuses her of acting like "a little white girl" crying rape. His outrage is, however, indefensible since he has in fact just launched an attack on her which is sexualized if not physical.

He has not only reduced her accomplishments to a set of favors traded for sexual access, but he has an understanding of the situation which explicitly pits her interests against his. Her dreams of gold, cloisonné, and honey-colored silk, which can be seen to represent her aspirations to financial success, artistic achievement, and the luxury of positive self-definition, are contrasted with his dreams of "black ladies in white dresses minding the pie table in the basement of the church."[11] The implication is that if Jadine cannot be the kind of black lady that Son the traditionalist can recognize then she cannot, indeed, be a black lady.

Examining the structural parallels between Margaret Street and Jadine exposes the shared ground between black and white men and thus reveals fissures along the lines of gender which suggests some of the ways in which black women's social and political interests may deviate from those articulated in the general discourse of the black counter public. The novel's rendering of physical containment and the discourse of sexual contamination as mutual elements structuring the lives of both Jadine and Margaret, undermines a simplistic reading of racial oppositions. These parallels work to demonstrate the degree to which Jadine's experience of blackness is simultaneously informed by her position as a woman. However, in contrast to Margaret, Jadine finds that by pushing back against racial definitions of her identity she can also expand the range of options available to her as a woman. Since the only privileges to which Margaret has access come to her as a result of her racial, rather than gender, identity, she has little recourse against the strictures of gender. On the other hand, the gender experience of the black woman is one of double alienation both from the racial privileges of whiteness and from the masculine privileges of blackness. In choosing to act against the traditional norms of blackness, Jadine expands the possibilities available to her. She denies anyone else the right to "get away with telling [her] what a black woman is or ought to be. . . ."[12]

THE SEARCH FOR NEW ARCHETYPES OF BLACK FEMININITY

Jadine's refusal to submit to others' definition of who she should be is best illustrated by an examination of her encounter with the Woman in Yellow, who, along with Son's black ladies minding pie tables, has been read as a symbol of ideal black femininity. Such readings are clearly responding to the dimensions of the novel which are situated in the long historical view and thus seek to recognize the centrality of the black woman to African American cultural vitality. However, those readings frequently dismiss the unresolved tensions that emerge from the intersection of ideal black femininity and the socio-reality of black femininity in the immediate post–civil rights era. In this section I want to suggest an alternative reading that presents their encounter as indicative of the need for new images of black femininity that reflect the social realities of the immediate post–civil rights moment. Such realities are the "stuff" of which the novel's popular aesthetic is made.

Her encounter with the Woman in Yellow, which predates the action of the novel, is recalled at the beginning of the second chapter and serves to establish the tension of negotiating the traditional requirements of black female identity. The initial confrontation between Jadine and the Woman in Yellow establishes oppositions of character that will continue to be examined throughout the novel. However, the fact that the Woman in Yellow is not a character but a symbol bears examination.

In the passage in which Jadine's memory of the Woman in Yellow is recounted, she is certainly framed as Jadine's ideological and physical antithesis. Her beauty, which is "too" excessive (or alien to Eurocentric standards of beauty) to be either adorned by eyelashes or be the object of photography or other forms of visual art, is contrasted with the dominant culture's acceptance of Jadine. However, two things complicate a strictly binaristic reading of the passage as merely a commentary on black women's exclusion from ideals of feminine beauty in Western culture. First, the passage actually aligns the Woman in Yellow with icons of white femininity which make Jadine anxious and destabilize her sense of self. The memory of the encounter with the Woman in Yellow is "a picture that was not a dream" which replaces the nightmare of Norma Shearer, Mae West, and Jeannette McDonald's flowered, feathered, and veiled hats which initially disturbed Jadine's consciousness. By connecting the two oppositions—physical ideals of white femininity and the cultural ideals of black femininity—the passage marks twin prongs of Jadine's alienation as a post–civil rights black woman who is positioned to challenge both ideals. In contrasting the reality and the dream, though, the passage also suggests that her immediate historical circumstance may have more of an impact on Jadine's sense of self.

Given that the opposition to white female standards of beauty is an age-old experience for African American women and given her obvious success as model, the anxiety produced by comparing herself to Eurocentric standards may be experienced as less potent than that called up by comparing herself with traditional standards of black female identity. Thus, the emphasis on the reality of the event over the interpretation of the dream suggests its greater significance in Jadine's life. This question of reality and significance brings us to the second important way the passage exceeds a binaristic staging of the conflict between black and white standards of beauty. The surrealistic nature of the episode which Jadine recalls works to destabilize the authority of the Woman in Yellow and the ideological position that she is understood to represent.

In her very provocative essay, "The Gender of Diaspora in *Tar Baby*," Yogita Goyal elucidates the novel's interrogation of gender relations in the context of diaspora, shedding light on the ideological work assigned to women's bodies in this text. She identifies two levels of narration at work in the novel. She argues that the mythic level of narration is used to present a unitary notion of the diaspora which is symbolized through the feminized landscape of the Caribbean, the nurturing values associated with Son, and most of the actual black women in the text, all of whom are positioned in opposition to Jadine. On the other hand, the historically situated truth of fissures along lines of race, class and geography are presented in a realist mode, which "indicates a skepticism about the value of tradition, particularly in its relation to constructions of gender, and offers alternative ways of negotiating the modern world."[13] While Goyal focuses on the way that gendered discourses reveal schisms within the diaspora, her exposure of the centrality of historical orientation is most suggestive for my analysis, since the tension between the two historical orientations to blackness is the primary distinction I am drawing between the popular and the literary.

In tying together media images of iconic white women, a symbol of black female cultural identity, and Jadine's self-image, the novel taps into the era's zeitgeist. It suggests the diminished salience of white images and the need to reformulate black identity ideals. Because it lacks the same history of communal support that opposing white standards of femininity enjoys, that challenge that Jadine launches against traditional notions of black femininity feels much more fraught with danger. It is in fact what she finds after probing for "the center of the fear" she feels when confronted with the dream of the hats.[14] The suggestion then is that the true source of that which "shamed and repelled her so" is her move away from traditional black femininity rather than any failure to live up to a white ideal. Nonetheless, the two notions of femininity are for Jadine, as they are for many black women of the post–civil rights era, intimately connected, as her nighttime musings indicate. Jadine's quest for a resonant black female image links geography and gender ideology in some ways that complicate the socio-reality of the black public culture debate's shift from rural focus to urban concerns.

It is important to keep in mind that Jadine's dream/memory is in fact activated by Son's attempt to manipulate her consciousness. The night of her dream would have been one of those nights, of which the reader belatedly learns, when Son would stealthily enter her room and focus his thoughts in an effort to make her "lie still and dream steadily the dreams he wanted her to have about yellow houses with white doors" and black women standing in front of them shouting "Come on in, you honey you!"[15] His dreams are primarily shaped by the romance of the South as the authentic source of African American culture and values but also bear the imprint of Black Nationalist discourse in the emphasis on Eloe as an independent black township. Son's description of his hometown, Eloe, conveniently omits that this township is in fact intimately connected to the white world which "pumps the water, hooks up the telephones" and otherwise provides the basic infrastructure on which the town depends.[16]

In this way, his account of Eloe echoes black separatist rhetoric, the most immediate discourse of the historical period in which the novel is set. As Son's narrative of an independent and egalitarian Eloe ignores its positioning within a larger framework, so too did the rhetoric of Black Nationalism. While Son minimizes the town's connection to a material infrastructure, Nationalist discourses focus on black masculine authority without acknowledging that its patriarchal narrative reproduces the gender relations of the dominant culture. Jadine's refusal to accept his narrative of completely independent black community challenges the idealization of rural black culture and her experiences in Eloe, which I discuss later, expose its reactionary gender politics.

In contrast to Nationalism's phallocentric concept of black liberation, *Tar Baby* puts the black woman at the center of its inquiry into the experience of black social freedom. In the Woman in Yellow dream memory Morrison creates a triptych of female identities which uses Jadine to interrogate the very real question of how the twenty-first-century black woman will negotiate the past and future of black identity and experience. The various women—her mother, the Woman in Yellow, Aunt Rosa—that Jadine identifies as the night women, are allies in Son's particular brand of patriarchal black masculinity. As J. Brooks Bouson points out, "even as the narrative directs reader to determine that Jadine is shamed because she has denied her essential femaleness, it also, in part, subverts this message by presenting the night women as a shameful, if not grotesque, spectacle and as embodiments of a stigmatizing difference."[17] Jadine's difference from these women is a very specific difference marked by varying regional and temporal differences.

It is their particular mode of blackness to which Jadine objects, not black femaleness in general; she has no ambivalence or hesitation regarding those who serve to expand her possibilities as a black woman. In fact she is identified with the mode of black femininity she witnesses in New York, where female power is measured in relation to professional achievement and positioning rather than the reproduction of black masculinity. Thus, she chooses the urban over the rural, mobility over rootedness, individuality over community, in spite of the way that they are discursively positioned as antithetical to black wholeness and authenticity. As Yogita Goyal has noted, Jadine's choices help to unpack the hidden gender scripts buried in the discourse of blackness. Honing in on Son as a figure that represents nationalist discourses, she reminds us that "Nationalist discourses are widely credited with a certain fetishization of women as sign of an authentic cultural identity in the name of tradition."[18] In rejecting all of the markers of traditional black experience—ruralism, a focus on origins, and a communal ethic—Jadine strategically chooses values which allow her to forge a different kind of black woman's experience.

Shifting our critical approach—from a "traditional" African Americanist perspective oriented to accounting for a coherent African American experience, to popular literature's more precisely historicized perspective and concern with dialogic approaches to African American identity—behooves the critic to pay more attention to that which is revealed by the juxtaposition of Jadine and the Woman in Yellow. Reading these two characters in geographically and historically situated ways opens up new possibilities of understanding this novel's engagement of black femininity in the post–civil rights era by pitting reality against myth. As Goyal argues, the Woman in Yellow belongs to the world of myth, while Jadine belongs to the world of reality. If myth and reality are marked by opposing narrative styles, as Goyal argues, they are also associated with varying geographies. Paris and New York are the geographies of the post–civil rights black woman while Isle de Chevaliers and Eloe are the sites of a mythological world of male superiority. In Paris, we see Jadine as an individual black woman exploring the newly available opportunities of the post–civil rights generation. If the (presumably African) Woman in Yellow existed in the novel as a real character and sociological representative of the immigrant African woman, rather than as a symbol, would it not be likely that she and Jadine would exist in sympathy rather than antipathy? Would she not, likely, be there to pursue similar economic and educational opportunities? Would she not likely be a member of her own nation's elite class? In thinking about what purpose, beyond highlighting Jadine's "inauthenticity," might be served by the Woman in Yellow's appearance in the Supramart in the nineteenth arrondissement, one must consider the shifts made possible by the political achievements of black people around the globe.

In the United States this expansion of opportunities along racial lines was also accompanied by shifts in the economic order, which proved favorable to African American women and precipitated an unprecedented examination of the role of black women in the popular cultural sphere.[19] This context, I think, greatly informs Jadine's encounter with the Woman in Yellow and marks it as a moment which focalizes the discursive examination that is taking place in the culture. While the text emphasizes her "unphotographable beauty,"[20] it also draws attention to her as both a spectacular and spectral presence; Jadine and the other patrons in the store gaze upon her without inhibition, hoping that as she exited the store she would "float through the glass the way a vision should."[21] Together with the gold tracks her sandals leave on the floor, such details mark her as an alien and fantastic presence. Her image will haunt Jadine for much of the novel. However, since it is she and not Jadine who exists on the margins of even the novel's reality, it is not necessary to conclude that this haunting is an indictment of Jadine's choices. Rather, we can read this encounter as one that raises the question of whether it serves us to be beholden to the mythology of an historical monolithic black identity. The question of their relationship is shifted away from what Jadine has lost to one of how these two images of black femininity might coexist in the context of post–civil rights society. And it is this question, I would argue that many readers—especially newly emergent members of the black female middle class—would identify with.

One of the ways in which this novel's highly specified time period resonates is through the novel's references to mass media and black people's new prominence within them. The principal action of the novel is set in 1977 and 1978, a time which is marked by the emergence of a new technological and economic order and new opportunities for African American women. This milieu is captured in the text in Jadine's assessment of New York as a black woman's town. Jadine's perception is that

> If ever there was a black woman's town, New York was it. No, no, not over there making land-use decisions or deciding what was or was not information. But there, there, and there. . . . They refused loans at Household Finance, withheld unemployment checks and drivers' licenses, issued parking tickets and summonses. Gave enemas, blood transfusions and please lady don't make me mad. They jacked up meetings in boardrooms, turned out luncheons, energized parties, redefined fashion, tipped scales, removed lids, cracked covers,

and turned an entire telephone company into such a diamondhead of hostility the company paid you for not talking to their operators. . . . This would be her city too. . . .[22]

This passage captures perfectly the sense of novelty that accompanied black women's entry into new social spaces and the hunger for delineations of the force, of the contradictions, of the joy they engendered when they arrived.

Jadine's positive response to the city is tied to its status as a media capital and black women's positioning within those circuits of communication. Her reaction comes as no surprise since her success as model is a linchpin of the novel. Moreover, her response and her profession combined also reminds of the 1975 film *Mahogany*, which tells a similar story of interrupted romance between a black man and woman, because of her desire to see what she can achieve as a model in Europe. I would argue, though, that the social resonance is just as important as the plot echoes. *Mahogany* was the second film released by Motown Productions and a significant part of the emergence of black crossover films and an increased televisual presence in the 1970s. As a result, not just the film but the entire social context of the era is called to mind by the film.

In a provocative reading of the ways in which the film represents black female professional aspiration in "the context of the political, social, and racial dynamics of the early 1970s," Miriam Thaggert offers a number of insights about the film, *Mahogany*, which are salient to my reading of *Tar Baby*. Thaggert demonstrates that the image of the black female career woman presented in the film is in conversation with the ideology of black mobility, generally. Furthermore, her discussion of the importance of "visual aptitude"—the ability to effectively decipher and create meaning through images—to the characters' success hints at the growing importance of media literacy that is a direct result of the technological shifts which drive the emergence of the information economy that began in this era. While *Mahogany*'s resolution maybe as unsatisfying as that of *Tar Baby* since neither presents an ideal solution to "the difficulty of finding effective creative outlets [for black women]" while simultaneously meeting the "need for a fulfilling personal life with an admirable partner," both texts speak eloquently to important aspects of the "dilemmas of post–civil rights black female life."[23]

Morrison's Jadine, like the fictional Tracy Chambers of *Mahogany*, must be read in light of the black liberation discourse of the immediate post–civil rights era in which black nationalist ideology "appropriated the black matriarchy concept to assert a heterosexual, masculine dominance as a vital component to the black revolution."[24] In light of the prominence of such discourse, Jadine's antipathy toward the Woman in Yellow—and, indeed, toward all of the "night women" who make her feel both naked and insufficient—must be read as more than mere assimilation. In reproducing readings which position Jadine again and again as one who has lost touch with her blackness, critics echo Son's logic—she will behave in ways that we understand as recognizably black, or we will not acknowledge her as one of the community. However, if we read Jadine as a character who represents a specific moment in the historical experience of African American women, we can begin to understand that she functions in many ways as the archetype of twenty-first century black femininity and the newfound prominence of the black woman in specific labor markets, media imagery, and even symbolically in the immediate post–civil rights moment. Moreover, I want to suggest that reading her against the grain of black women's tradition and in relation to other cultural images of black femininity helps to free her from the binary notion of black identity and to see her character as progenitor of a new set of black female images.

JADINE AS PROTOTYPICAL CULTURAL MULATTO

Though the question of what kind of woman Jadine is was one that initially bewildered much of the critical audience for this text, the passage of time and the insights of theorists of contemporary African American literature have supplied us with a name for a phenomenon such as Jadine—the cultural mulatto. The cultural mulatto is an archetype which foregrounds post–civil rights historicity and invites multiple interpretation rather than offering static or singular formulations of black identity. In fact, theorists and practitioners of the post-soul aesthetic have located ambiguity and fluidity as the ur-conditions of contemporary blackness and have embraced the possibilities for more complex understandings of a variegated blackness that result from examining black culture alongside white culture instead of in opposition to it. As such, reading Jadine as a pro-typical cultural mulatto proves enabling. It allows the reader to perceive the inaccuracy of historical constructions of white and black culture as completely separate as well as to see how the cultural mulatto figure redounds with particular sexual implications for the black woman.

From the initial articulation of the concept in 1989 to the present, the post-soul aesthetic has pointed us toward a recognition of the way African-Americans are deeply influenced by the artifacts and attitudes of a presumably white American culture;[25] of the way in which soul as a metaphor for black culture rests on a masculinist notion of black identity which shapes it largely in relation to capitalist/heterosexist/patriarchal norms;[26] and of the necessity of dismantling monolithic notions of blackness to cultivate a space of freedom for the black artist and individual.[27] This orientation toward blackness as relational rather than strictly oppositional has proved for some a dismaying notion with the result that many texts evincing the post-soul aesthetic have been ignored at best, and excoriated at worst. Critics have assumed that failure to reproduce a presumed black tradition equates with a complete rejection of that tradition.

Moving away from this assumption opens up a number of productive approaches to interpreting Jadine Child's attitudes and actions. Her relationship to white culture is, in fact, at the heart of those readings which align her with the loss of authentic black identity. Jadine's educational attainment, along with her physical appearance, indict her to Son and many readers, as well. Such suspicion reflects the inheritance of certain intra-racial attitudes which position the black woman and the educated "Negro" as suspects of treacherous alliances with the white power structure. Indeed, one of the most repeated phrases in the scholarship on *Tar Baby* must be the observation of "Jadine's uncritical acceptance of white European culture and values."[28]

Two passages which are frequently cited as evidence of her cultural assimilation. One is that in which she wonders whether her French boyfriend will continue to be attracted to her when he discovers that she's bored by Mingus, doesn't like hoop earrings, and prefers Ave Maria to gospel music. In other words that she is perhaps not very culturally different from him, or from white American culture. The second article of evidence against her is her assertion that Picasso's visual interpretations of Itumba mask are better than the originals, or as she says, "proof of his genius, not the mask maker's."[29] Looking at those statements in context belies the idea that Jadine has no racial consciousness. After all, her ambivalence about accepting the offer of marriage from her boyfriend, Ryk, has to do with her awareness that, perhaps, his interest in her is motivated by some racialist notion of the exotic black women—a role she refuses. Similarly, her rejection of Itumba mask is a response to the liberal politics of Michael Street, heir to the Valerian Street's empire. Her rejection of the "primitive" counters his idealization of it when he counsels her to return to Philadelphia's Morgan Street to experience the "thrill" of making "African" pots for barter.[30]

Given that each of her claims to European culture is a response to what Jadine perceives as someone else's attempt to define for her what it means to be black, I understand them to reflect an attempt to carve out a space for white culture within the parameters of blackness, rather than an outright rejection of blackness. Furthermore, that the responses are to white male attempts to construct her as exotic is important given Jadine's status as an ascriptive mulatta—that is, as one whose honey skin, minky eyes, and wavy hair are celebrated markers of black female desireability. Her challenge to this exoticization highlights her subjection to both race and gender stereotypes. It also challenges over-determined readings of her attitudes by disrupting the tendency to read black identity as merely cultural rather than mutually constituted by gender, class, and other categories of experience.

To read her preferences as anti-black elides the fact that black and white cultural forms have existed in synthetic relationship for as long as black and white people have been in contact with each other. To define classical music as strictly white ignores a long history of African American participation in the field of classical music, the consistency with which Ave Maria has appeared in the repertoire of African American divas, and the reality that musical taste is a coincidence of personal experience. In other words, while European classical music clearly has its origins in the aesthetics of the continent, it cannot be said to belong solely to white people, given the collective and individual efforts black people have made to legitimate their presence in the field. If we are not going to take to task such black artists as Marian Anderson or Jessye Norman for their implicit preference for this kind of music, then to make it a central piece of evidence in the case of Jadine's supposed black self-hatred can only be understood as a willfully myopic reading strategy which results in the perpetuation of an exclusionary notion of black identity.

By contrast, my reading of Jadine as a cultural mulatto enables a dual challenge. Her physical embodiment as an (ascriptive) mulatto lays bare the lie on which the notion of distinct black and white cultures is based. As Bertram Ashe notes, the reality of shared experience across racial lines is frequently expressed in the trope of the cultural mulatto. This figure is one who may not be a biologically "mixed" but whose "multi-racial mix" of cultural experiences means that she can "navigate easily in the white world" as part of her blackness.[31] The radical potential of the cultural mulatto lies in the willingness to acknowledge white culture as part of blackness. Still, a less productive aspect of the cultural mulatto as symbol is obscured by the emphasis on culture over biology. On one hand, Jadine' experience illustrates the cultural mulatto figure's value for thinking about and acknowledging the syncretic nature of African American cultural identity. As a type, the cultural mulatto destabilizes any notion of a monolithic black culture by recalling the extent to which intermixture has figured prominently in the development of African American cultural forms, from music and dance to language and food. On the other hand, Jadine's experience also illuminates how framing the mulatto figure with an emphasis on culture over biology can erase important dimensions of how the concept of mulattism has historically operated.

For the female, in particular, the status of mulatta has been interwoven with oppressive ideologies of sexuality and gender. In the Caribbean as well as in parts of the United States, such as Louisiana, elaborate systems of social hierarchy emerged in which mixed-race women occupied a distinct social strata predicated on severing them from their "black" counterparts, reserving their sexual availability for white male consumption, and extending to them some privileges of economic and social mobility. The figure of the mulatta has been simultaneously invested with degrading notions of sexual availability and the exaltation of white normative feminine appearance. As a consequence, the black woman whose physical and cultural experiences are marked by the mulatto intermixture encounters additional challenges in enacting the role of cultural mulatto. She is rendered suspect by this history of sexual exchange and comes to represent an assault on the privileges of black masculinity, rather than being a symbol of the fluidity of black culture. For example, this history is registered during Jadine's visit to Eloe with Son. In Eloe—Son's hometown and the Garden of Eden of Blackness—Jadine is repeatedly subjected to the sexualizing gaze of its residents. When Son's Aunt Rosa discovers that Jadine has been sleeping in the nude her look is powerful enough to make Jadine's nakedness a living thing that " . . . lay down with her" making her feel "More than exposed. Obscene."[32] Extending this sexualized gaze, Son's friends look at her "like she was a Cadillac he had won, or stolen, or even bought for all they knew."[33] Each of these viewers constructs her sexuality as debased without any interaction beyond their looking. The ease with which they associate her with prostitution or other "loose" forms of sexuality reflects the legacy of the discourse of mulatta sexual wantoness. Her experience in Eloe demonstrates the gendered dimensions of narratives of black cultural authenticity. Collectively, the various identities that others attempt to impose on her fuel Jadine's quest to locate enabling spaces and models of femininity. In pursuing these goals she embodies, for the reader, the very thing that she seeks.

CONCLUSION

Jadine's dilemma of identity stems from the struggle to reconcile her Self to iconic notions of blackness formulated in a social context in which white and black cultural norms and practices were perceived to be overarching and entirely separate. As a member of the first generation to feel it had direct and legitimate access to "American" (i.e. white cultural norms and experience), Jadine is called upon to chart new territory in terms of how to formulate an identity that synthesizes aspects of white culture along with launching the traditional oppositions and critiques. Moreover, her position also reveals the way that the post–civil rights era necessitates the same kind of examination process regarding blackness. To read the Woman in Yellow as merely a symbol of Jadine's loss of some authentic identity is to fail to see the deliberate choices she undertakes (rather than just laboring under false consciousness) and more importantly to see the ways in which Morrison's text actually supports Jadine's skeptical approach. Morrison simultaneously idealizes the night women and sets them in opposition to Jadine's desire to express herself artistically and nurture her own sexuality and professional capacities. The tension between these two paths of femininity is most forcefully expressed through the Woman in Yellow's surreal intrusion into Jadine's celebration of self on the occasion of being chosen for the cover of *Elle* at the same time that she is being glamorously pursued by "three gorgeous and raucous men" and is in receipt of a letter confirming that her exam for the Master's in Art History was satisfactorily completed.

In light of such tension, it seems absurd to simply read Jadine as a symbol of cultural loss. Levying charges of assimilationist cultural self-loathing ignores a number of important facts. The first is that to a certain extent, access to Euro-American culture was at least a partial goal of the civil rights movement and a certain goal of Uncle Sydney's request on behalf of his niece. Second, and more importantly, such statements ignore the fact that Jadine is selective and perhaps even strategic regarding which aspects of European culture and values she adopts. She is shown to have a clear critical consciousness regarding racial stereotypes and the hierarchies they support, whether they emanate from the white community or black.

Moreover, Morrison's use of aspects of romantic fiction works to further destabilize traditional interpretations of the novel. By featuring a glamorous self-contained world that emphasizes personal and individual desire, Morrison uses elements of the popular romance to elicit an emotional response from readers, thereby contributing to the dialogic character of the novel. Presenting us with a character who lives a fast-paced, adventurous life, vacationing in private homes on private Caribbean islands and socializing with actresses and models who maintain homes on both coasts creates an impact that would not be as forceful if she were, say, an administrative assistant struggling to pay her rent. It helps to create an identification with and sympathy for her character's reticence to settle for the more mundane life that Son would have her adopt. In light of nationalist understandings of black femininity as self-sacrificing, as rooted, and as reproductive, her ambition, her mobility, the choices Jadine makes are of great significance. Her rejection of origins or motherhood and, most of all, her final choice, make her a character like no other in the canon of African American female characters. As Trudier Harris so wisely noted, "African American folk culture has not prepared us well for a female outlaw. . . ."[34] If we approach a reading of this novel from a popular literature orientation, the possibility of a less ambivalent reading emerges. Jadine's actions and attitudes become space-clearing moments which acknowledge the cleavages in black identity along lines of nation, class, and gender with which real life women grapple every day.

NOTES

1. See Stuart Hall's essay "Cultural Identity and Diaspora" In *Colonial Discourse and Post-Colonial Theory*, ed. Patrick Williams and Laura Chrisman, 392–403. New York: Columbia University Press, 1994.

2. Ibid., 56.

3. Ibid., 75.

4. Toni Morrison, *Tar Baby*, 55.

5. Ibid., 56.

6. Ibid., 155.

7. Ibid., 82.

8. Ibid., 120.

9. Ibid., 119.

10. Ibid., 120.

11. Ibid., 119.

12. Morrison, 121.

13. Yogita Goyal, "The Gender of Diaspora in *Tar Baby*," *Modern Fiction Studies* 52, no. 2 (2006): 394.

14. Toni Morrison, *Tar Baby*, 44.

15. Ibid., 119.

16. Ibid., 172.

17. J. Brooks Bouson, *Quiet as It's Kept: Shame, Trauma, and Race in the Novels of Toni Morrison*, (Albany: State University of New York Press, 2000), 123.

18. Goyal, 397.

19. For a discussion of how the rise of the information technology sector opened up new labor opportunities for women of color see Cynthia Fuch Epstein and Stephen R. Duncombe's "Women Clerical Workers" in *Dual City: Restructuring New York*. New York: Russell Sage Foundation, 1991.

20. Morrison, *Tar Baby*, 46.

21. Ibid., 46.

22. Ibid., 222.

23. Miriam Thaggert, "Marriage, Moynihan, Mahagony: Success and the Post–Civil Rights Black Female Professional in Film," *American Quarterly* 64, no. 4 (2012): 737.

24. Ibid., 731.

25. See Trey Ellis's "The New Black Aesthetic."

26. This is an argument Mark Anthony Neal lays out in the introduction to *Post-Soul Babies*. It is also cogently discussed in Robin Kelley's essay "Lookin' for the Real Nigga."

27. Thelma Golden offers this line of argument in her introduction to the catalog for the 2001 exhibit "Freestyle" which she curated for the Harlem Studio Museum. Bertram Ashe follows a similar line of reasoning in his introduction to *African American Review*'s special issue on post-soul aesthetics, which he edited in 2007.

28. Malin Walther Pereira, "Periodizing Toni Morrison's Work from The Bluest Eye to Jazz," *MELUS* 22, no. 3 (1997): 71–82.

29. Toni Morrison, *Tar Baby*, 74

30. Ibid., 73.

31. Quoted in Ashe, "Introduction," 613.

32. Morrison, 253.

33. Ibid., 254.

34. Trudier Harris, *Fiction and Folklore: The Novels of Toni Morrison* (Knoxville: University of Tennessee Press, 1991), 128.

Chapter Three

Girlfriend Fiction

Black Women Writers and Readers Negotiating Post–Civil Rights Womanhood

In her book *Black Women as Cultural Readers* Jacqueline Bobo illuminates how black women, as audiences for various forms of literary and filmic representations, read in ways that provoke useful dialogue and facilitate a discourse of black female resistance. In one instance, she cites an intriguing explanation of Terry McMillan's popularity as proffered by one of the interview subjects: "I'll tell you why she's selling. Because she's just like one of us sitting here talking about all the stuff that we usually talk about."[1] This statement offers an intriguing point of entry to the concerns of this chapter because, like Bobo, I am deeply interested in understanding how black women as writers and readers establish their own autonomous perspectives on contemporary black life and experience. As I have established in the previous chapters, the critic of African American literature plays an essential role in shaping our understanding of the forms, themes, and tropes which constitute a distinctly African American literary approach. I have also alluded to the idea that lay readers also have an important place in the shaping of African American literary production. In this chapter I would like to explore that idea more fully by examining some examples of the ways in which Girlfriend literature (of the late 1990s and early 2000s) engages public discourses regarding black women. The significance of such responses is linked to the way that they position the social priorities of an African American reading public on an equal plane with black political concerns as defined in the academy. As a result, this genre represents an important mechanism of black women's participation in the black public sphere.

By the end of the twentieth century, the sorry state of black women's romantic affairs had become a hot topic in print and television news reportage, the self-help publishing industry, and in the private conversations of upwardly mobile black women, in particular. From Shahrazad Ali's publication of the *Blackman's Guide to Understanding the Blackwoman* in 1989 to ABC news' *Nightline* coverage of the topic beginning in 2009, the "problem" of the chronically single black woman has been endlessly rehashed in the public sphere. Black feminist critics in the fields of political science and cultural studies have offered useful critiques of the way in which these narratives of the black woman are linked to both historical and contemporary constructions of black sexuality in American political culture.

However, as black women's perspectives tend to be discredited because of the perception of black women as racially treacherous, overly ambitious, and aggressively emotional, their ability to "forcefully and convincingly advocate their own interest in the public sphere—either in black political movements or in American policy environments" has, according to Melissa Harris-Perry, been limited.[2] Recognizing the limits of their positioning within traditional intellectual locales many black women have sought out other spheres of public life from which to mobilize. It is my contention that the realm of popular literary production is one that black women have consciously sought to exploit by centralizing social experience-based themes. In the production of popular literature black women have found a platform from which to challenge the authority of a literary establishment ill-equipped to address the complexities of black women's experience in the post–civil rights era.

In *Communion: The Female Search for Love*, bell hooks argues that in the absence of formal engagement of a specific social need, popular cultural forms that do address the topic will emerge. She offers the following illustration:

> The feminist movement had launched a devastating critique at conventional ways of thinking about heterosexual love and romance, but it had not encouraged the development of new theories and publication of numerous books on the subject of love—books that would have illuminated for us how to make abiding, joyous relationships in the context of patriarchal culture. Stepping into the gap, the place where masses of women, irrespective of our sexual preferences, were registering unhappiness with love, self-help books (most of which were non-feminist) offered direction and guidance.[3]

Likewise, it is my assertion that black women's popular fiction is generating a discourse on black female experience in the post–civil rights era that addresses those very specific anxieties around class and romance which have not made it to the center of public debates regarding contemporary black experience. For instance, while black feminist criticism has done much to bring black women's experience into focus, it has done so in a way that centers on challenging the historical representation of African American women as a collective and seeks "to eradicate the harmful and pervasive images haunting their history."[4] Conversely, popular fiction tends to focus on the experiences of women as individuals and in the present. The themes and tropes that are developed in this body of literature deserve our attention because they capture a unique historical moment. At no other time in history have black women wielded so much professional authority, nor have the social norms and aesthetics associated with the black working class, as in the case of hip hop culture, been so widely assimilated into general culture. For the critic of African American literature to continue to ignore those perspectives which emerge from the class and gender margins is really to ignore reality. In turn, s/he can be said to be failing to advance the professional mission of elucidating an art which is largely understood as an index of African American social experience.

In addition to their diverging temporal orientations, accounts of black female experience emerging from traditional, institutional perspectives and from popular cultural locales differ in the degree to which they cleave to tradition—aesthetically or conceptually. Though black feminist perspectives rooted in the academy and those emerging from the other cultural spheres may exhibit overlapping perspectives, they tend to engage the issues in very distinctive ways. In thinking about the emergence of Girlfriend fiction as part of the black public sphere, we must consider that literature by African American women had just recently become institutionalized within the academy. Black feminist criticism had, as I describe in chapter one, established that there was a tradition of literary endeavor by African American women. In addition to identifying some tropes that would come to be seen as central to African American literary endeavor, the unearthing of such a tradition also revealed how African American women had used their art to insert their specific concerns as women into the larger discourse on African American freedom. In centralizing the literary arts as a viable strategy for black women to represent their own interest within the black community, this moment would provide fertile ground for the flowering of a mass fiction movement among black women.

It was into this tradition that Terry McMillan—presently credited as the mother of Girlfriend fiction—attempted to assert herself along with contemporaries such as Alice Walker and Gloria Naylor. Initially, critics accepted such an alignment but as McMillan's work moved away from traditional black literary themes such as the struggle for economic stability captured in her first novel, *Mama*, treating her work as serious literature became less acceptable. As her work came to be characterized by more distinctly individualistic themes such as emotional vulnerability and self-doubt, her work also became more relevant in the marketplace; arguably reaching a peak from

1992 to 1996 with the publications of *Waiting to Exhale* and *How Stella Got Her Groove Back*, respectively. This fissure between critical interest and consumer interest is, in my estimation, a result of the critical reading practices that were established in academia alongside the development of black feminist criticism.

It is possible to argue that the lack of critical interest in these texts is entirely due to the lack of "artistic" quality. Critics often cite a lack of depth in the development of her characters, over reliance on profane language in the dialogue, and a tendency toward formulaic plot resolutions. Such an argument, however, would require that we ignore the preferences of mass fiction audiences who affirmed the value of her texts by buying them, lending them, and discussing them in unprecedented numbers.[5] In assessing audience responses, I think it is important to remember the game-changing nature of black women's entry in the marketplace. For example, in 1999 William Cook made claims that both the production and consumption of African American literature had been feminized. More recently, Herman Gray took note of "the commercial success and critical recognition of black writers, especially in the areas of black women's fiction, biography, and memoir" as part of the context for his broad analysis of the politics of contemporary black representation.[6]

Moreover, these audiences did so right in tandem with their purchasing, lending, and discussion of works by McMillan's more "serious" peers. Thus we must return to the comment with which this chapter opens, "she's just like one of us," which points us to the important role of identification in the success of McMillan's work and the genre of Girlfriend fiction as a whole. In other words, these texts integrate audiences into the narrative in ways which more traditional literature does not. Unfortunately, the same identification and integration that intrigues the reader presents an obstacle for the critic, who often failed to recognize the direct language as a mode of the vernacular at work in the text; the engagement of romance as an extension of coupling as a political subject within the African American community; or the affirmation of black women's self-interest as a challenge to the masculinist tenor of black liberation discourses.

My identification of the authority of the audience in the production of mass fiction or popular literature is rooted, ironically, in Henry Louis Gates's discussion of Signifyin' as a hallmark feature of African American literary practice. In *The Signifying Monkey*, Gates presents a description of African American literary practice in the eras of slavery and Jim Crow. He argues that literacy was a tool by which African American subjects asserted their humanity. In demonstrating their mastery of formal literacy, the African American author provided a counter-narrative to the general assumption of African American cultural inferiority. However, according to Gates, even as they exhibited their mastery of a Euro-American notion of literacy, they managed to marry to it a uniquely black aesthetic in the form of Signifyin'.

Rooted in the very oral tradition which was seen by the dominant culture as evidence of their inferiority, the power of Signifyin(g) rests in the fact that the production of meaning is shared between the speaker/author and the listener/reader. By contrast, traditional Euro-American literary approaches privilege a closed system wherein "signification depends for order and coherence on the exclusion of unconscious associations which any given word yields at any given time. . . ."[7] African American cultural Signification—denoted with the capital S—"luxuriates in the inclusion of the free play of these associative rhetorical and semantic relations" thus everything which, in the former mode, "must be excluded for meaning to remain coherent and linear comes to bear in the process. . . ."[8] This "Signfyin(g)" approach to language, then, creates a space for the reader to bring his or her own referents, experiential or otherwise, into the rhetorical field. As such, this theory of the black literary practice seems well suited to a genre in which the reader's role is explicitly acknowledged.

My explanation for the general critical failure to recognize Girlfriend literature and other popular forms as coextensive with the canon as it is presently constituted has everything to do with history. As discussed in chapter one, the theoretical perspectives presented in *The Signifying Monkey*, emerged at a highly politicized moment in the development of black studies. Given that both scholars of African descent and scholarly perspectives rooted in the unique assumptions of the black studies paradigm—that methodologies for examining black history and culture should reflect the unique aesthetics of that culture—were newly entered into the Euro-American academy, the scholars and the work they produced had to enact a very challenging balancing act. They needed, simultaneously, to demonstrate the cultural distinction of their subjects, mastery of a body of knowledge recognizable to their peers, and a political orientation that would not be perceived as too militant.

Thus, while the insights enabled by the notion of Signifyin' practices as a hallmark characteristic of African American literary production would seem to encompass a variety of styles and genres, its application led elsewhere. Instead of instantiating a tradition rooted in the politics and experience of the immediate post–civil rights era, critics produced a literary tradition that was rooted not in the stylistic and psychological autonomy of the black power era, but in the integrationist aesthetic of the nineteenth and early twentieth centuries. African American literary studies found itself in the position of having to prove its value to the white academy by demonstrating its internalization of the methods and aesthetics of the dominant culture. As a result a critical methodological paradigm emerged which actually mirrored the Structuralist assumptions which scholars of the era sought to critique. In the choices they made regarding which texts to anthologize, to teach, or to take up as subjects of criticism, they privileged those texts which, because they were primarily rooted in a Euro-American aesthetic yielded themselves to critical approaches also rooted in that aesthetic. Much of the scholarship of this period then enacts a methodology which inadvertently aligns it with critical assumptions against which the scholars were attempting to define African American literature. This method aligns with Gates's concept of signification, elaborated in *The Signifyin(g) Monkey*, in which a one-to-one relationship between the signifier and the signified exists. With this formulation, Gates pointed to the ideological function of language, suggesting how the concept of formal literacy extends beyond adherence to conventions of grammar or the means of transmission. The formalist, dominant cultural approach relies on linguistic complexity, logical abstraction, and symbolic imagery rather than centralizing clarity and directness of language. In this way the author excludes the possibility of multiple meanings and retains control of the process of signification. Consequently, applying such a method to texts which consciously aim to speak to and speak for its audience in the language of that audience, subverts the very goal of establishing a shared interpretive community.

The analysis of the popular titles, *The Hand I Fan With* by Tina Ansa; *The Interruption of Everything* by Terry McMillan; and Bebe Moore Campbell's *72 Hour Hold* which follows represents my attempt to evaluate this literature on its own terms and to demonstrate that this literature constitutes an intervention in black public life. In thinking about the literature as intervening in the public sphere, I am building on Herman Gray's notion of cultural moves. These moves, or trends of attitude and perception, may seem to arise organically but are in fact institutionally constituted through the participation of artists, intellectuals, and critics; all of whom play an important role in conferring legitimacy, prestige, and recognition on the products which constitute black commercial culture.[9] By drawing attention to the role of the audience also plays in legitimizing the very vital facet of black commercial culture that is Girlfriend fiction, I mean to highlight the extra-institutional influence that they wield. This impact can be seen in both the themes and the aesthetics which characterize the genre.

By examining a literature which has been embraced by black consumers but largely ignored by black cultural producers, my goal in this chapter is to show how popular women writers have offered their own interpretations of how late twentieth century African American women negotiated issues such as economic stratification in the black community, the tension between self-care, self-sacrifice, and the reemergence of narratives of black female deviance from the norms of femininity. Additionally, I want to take up the issue of how black women writers' strategic use of the conventions of Girlfriend fiction—the happy ending, narrative accessibility, and common, reality-based situations—to speak back to and broaden the account of black women's experience which emerges from more canonical perspectives. This relatively simple structure does not automatically limit the impact of these works. Instead, readers are afforded a crucial role in making meaning of these texts because they are able to bring to bear the associative referents of their own experiences and it allows for the experience of pleasure in communal narration that Bobo's respondents articulate when they discuss McMillan's work. They suggest that what draws them in is the fact that her characters find themselves in the very situations in which they have found themselves and those situations are presented "just like we would say it."[10]

In light of the constraints placed upon black women's attempts to "tell it like it is" in more traditional public arenas, it is crucial that we recognize their strategic use of print media as a means of gaining access to a public platform. In this fictional space, the characteristic themes emerge from very specific historical moment in the late twentieth century. At this time, a backlash against black social advances had emerged in the form of anti-affirmative action campaigns. These assaults were accompanied by two highly divergent popular images of black women—the crack mother and the female Buppie—both of which implicitly served as a justification for a rollback on affirmative policies for black social progress. The crack mother was "proof" of black cultural deviance and the futility of such policies while the Buppie was supposed to demonstrate that such policies were so effective they were no longer necessary. In Girlfriend fiction and other genres, black women writers of the era engaged the messy middle-ground of reality between these two poles. They developed stories which put the Buppie and the crack mother in dialogue or which probed beneath the surface of Buppie success to examine its cost. In this way, they contribute much to our understanding of public discourses of black identity from a female perspective.

THE HAND I FAN WITH AND THE SINGLE BLACK PROFESSIONAL

The Hand I Fan With provides an account of the adult Lena McPherson, protagonist of Ansa's debut novel *Baby of the Family*. In *Hand*, Lena is no longer a baby; her parents are dead, she has inherited "The Place," her father's bar, and has established a real estate business on her own. The adult Lena typifies the post–civil rights professional black woman; she's educated, affluent, and a bulwark within her community. The narrative draws attention to the consequences of such a position of power, registering in its delineation of the character's alienation, the ambivalence with which black women's relative empowerment has met. In this way, Lena McPherson represents an aspect of black women's experience that is unique to the post–civil rights era.

Lest we miss its engagement with the conflicted experience of the post–civil rights era, the novel begins by establishing the negative consequences of the social reorganization of U.S. society after civil rights legislation. Surveying the downtown area surrounding her office, she thinks that the downtown she once knew "looked as if it had taken a direct hit from a passing tornado . . . few structures were left standing in the area that had once been the bustling center of Mulberry, Georgia and the very heart of black folks' community in the small town since its establishment two hundred years before."[11] The emphasis on the degradation of this community echoes the general view that an unexpected consequence of integration has been the fragmentation and erosion of African American community.

Though the novel is a romance in which Lena McPherson, a financially successful, socially committed, and physically attractive black woman, has a love affair with a ghost, the introduction emphasizes the degree to which her experience reflects a specific social reality. Lena's wealth—established by descriptions of her luxurious home, fabulous wardrobe, and extreme largess within her community—offers an interesting juxtaposition to the wealth more commonly associated with pre-civil rights African American culture. In the 1960s, for instance, Nikki Giovanni wrote that black love is black wealth. As black women's independent access to material wealth has increased, the relatively stable love and family relationships which Giovanni's poem describes and names as wealth, have, apparently, become less and less accessible for middle-class African American women. Given the realities of today, where as many as one-third of young African American males are enmeshed in the prison system and the majority of the college degrees in the black community are earned by women, the expectation for the kind of relationships Giovanni refers to seems more and more fantastic.[12]

Just as Ann Petry's novel *The Street* registered black women's particular experience of racist exclusion from the capitalist order, this novel refracts the ambivalences of black mobility from an explicitly gendered perspective. As a consequence, it can be read as an important commentary on the ways in which black women's success in this era is constrained by the alienation it commonly produces. That Lena, like so many real women, has only "a ghost of a chance" at a satisfying romantic relationship opens an important space for the reader to bring her own experiences to bear in the narrative's interrogation of the profound psychic impact of the common social narrative of black women as unmarriageable. The novel offers a fantastical address of the problem which acknowledges the profundity of the dichotomy faced by the heterosexual African American woman while simultaneously providing readers with a narrative that challenges the implication that successful black women are inherently undesirable.[13] In other words, this use of the fantastic (Ansa's apparent respect for "alternative" or "traditional" belief systems aside) works along archetypal lines to validate the basic primal desire for an intimate emotional and physical connection. Although, by the end of the novel, Herman must return to the spirit world from which he has come, their relationship has affirmed that social power and sexual desirability in a women are not mutually exclusive.

Fantastic though it may be, the story of Lena McPherson's affair with Herman, the ghost whom she and her friend, Sister, conjure up using "things that Sister had from a ceremony she had attended at the International Yoruba Festival the year before, . . ." addresses the reality of contemporary African American women's struggle to achieve a balanced self-sufficiency.[14] Like many contemporary real-life African American women, Lena has a myriad of duties and, even as she performs one, others run through her head. In fact, she typifies those black women who, according to sociological accounts such as Donna Franklin's *What's Love Got to Do With It*, exhibit "high career expectations related to their perceptions of the expectations and desires of friends and family."[15] In spite of consistently meeting her professional and personal expectations and obligations, on occasion Lena feels that she would like to "just stand up in her own living room and scream" as a result of the burden of her commitments.[16] Though she has proven competent in meeting these perceived obligations, her own sense of value is undermined by the fact of her "chronic singleness." Echoing the dynamics of the contemporary discourse of successful black women as ineligible for marriage, the markers of Lena's success are converted to markers of alienation. As an adult woman the demons of her childhood—literal ghosts—have been transformed into "images of money and responsibility" to others, which "flew and danced and spun around her head into the wee hours" as the ghosts had previously.[17] Like the ghosts that haunted her childhood, these new ghosts also produce self-doubt in Lena.

Central to Lena's management of these new ghosts will be the arrival of Herman, an embodied spirit who will help her to relieve the "loneliness and confusion and weariness" that are so apparently incompatible with her success.[18] Prior to Herman's arrival, a primary obstacle for Lena is that with her gift of vision, she can never sustain a relationship because as physical intimacy increases the less savory aspects of "the man's thoughts and past came seeping out for Lena to hear and see right there. . . ."[19] These interruptions characterize all of her attempts at romance throughout her twenties and thirties before she concludes that she has little expectation for that particular kind of personal satisfaction. With repetition and the loss of hope Lena comes to focus on herself as the source of the problem, losing sight of the fact that in each case it was a man's "ugly secret" that presented the obstacle to their coupling. In fact, she so internalizes a sense of culpability that she comes to wonder if she is not divinely prohibited from enjoying an emotionally intimate relationship with a man because of her personal wealth. In church, after hearing the scripture "It is easier for a camel to go through the eye of a needle than for a rich man to enter the kingdom of heaven" she wonders if that explains why she has "a stunning pink short Chanel suit, a forty-foot indoor swimming pool, and heated stables, but no man, children or joy."[20] Though most women have neither Lena's wealth nor her ability to "see," many do, like Lena, find it difficult to keep "trying to forge on" in relationships with men who do not exhibit the honesty and kindness which they seek, and they wonder to what extent their success in other areas of their lives prohibits their success in the area of romantic relationships.[21] Donna Franklin, for instance, cites studies that suggest "the success of black women in the professions made it harder for them to maintain the traditional feminine role in relationships with their men."[22] Thus, the example of the male nurturer that the novel provides in the character of Herman, offers a hopeful symbol of alternative bases for organizing male female relationships.

In contrast to her previous experiences, Herman is deeply honest with Lena and takes Lena's pleasure as his purpose. That Herman is a ghost emphasizes the spiritual dimension of the relationship that Ansa is representing and prevents the narrative from slipping into the limited assumption of many romance stories—that a woman is not complete without a man. Just as Lena needs Herman, he needs her: "Lena was the focus of his revived life force. . . ."[23] In emphasizing the mutuality of their relationship—his embodiment depends on her recognition—and Herman's possession of characteristics from another day and age, Ansa suggests the degree to which African Americans need, in her own words, "to remember who we are and what we need to carry of ourselves into the next era."[24] Primary among these needs it would seem is the need to reconnect various constituents of the African-American community—male and female, young and old, rich and poor—without either group sacrificing itself to the other, as Lena ultimately learns through her relationship with Herman. In bridging oppositions such as past and present, Ansa's text creates a space for the contemporary reader in which her experience is linked to but not subsumed by the historical narrative.

THE INTERRUPTION OF EVERYTHING: BRIDGING THE SOCIO-ECONOMIC GAP

Terry McMillan and her work are probably the best known and most widely read of the three authors discussed here. Her personal biography has, apparently, deeply informed her body of work and certainly impacted the commercial reception of *The Interruption of Everything* which came on the heels of a much publicized break up of her marriage to Jonathan Plummer, the presumptive model for Winston Shakespeare of *How Stella Got Her Groove Back*. At the same time, scholarly and other critical attention to McMillan's work has been uneven. Though she has been publishing novels since 1987, not until 1998 did she begin to receive any significant attention from scholars of African American literature or Women's popular fiction.[25] At the same time, popular criticism of her work has, over the course of her career, been somewhat uneven. Generally she is praised and credited with having broken the ground from which the "Chick Lit" genre emerged, but some critics, such as *New York Times* reviewer Chelsea Cain, have seen her most recent work as predictable and lacking in subtlety and/or artistry.

Nonetheless, Paulette Richards's *Critical Companion* identifies themes, such as community and female social roles, which help to illuminate the emphatic response McMillan's work elicits from audiences. These themes along with the direct and, perhaps, unsubtle delineation of the characters in the novel make possible a direct identification on the part of the readers. The concrete recognition of the characters and situations creates a space for the reader, who, perhaps, provides the nuance herself from her own experience. Again, Bobo's work on and with black women's interpretive communities is useful. She suggests that as a result of reading from their own subjective positions, black women readers find and make meanings of texts that may not have been intended or even obvious to other readers. In discussing the responses of black women as an interpretive community to the film version of Alice Walker's *The Color Purple*, she notes that they exhibited a nuanced perspective that "complicated the widely held view that the film was a racist product directed by a racist director . . ." reframing the film "beyond its critical reception . . ." by focusing on those parts of it which were congruent with their own experience as well as their reading of the novel.[26] This interpretive approach is more communal, bringing the reader into the process along with the critic and the producer. The entire burden of meaning, then, does not rest on the author alone but creates space for the reader to participate in the process.

Typically work that merits the distinction of the "literary" appellation, exhibits a narrative approach in which the author has constructed a fictional world which is governed by a set of formal devices that reflect his or her own understanding of the social milieu out of which he or she writes. However, those very choices of metaphor, of narrative unfolding of time, of access to character psychology frame her understanding in a singular way, which ultimately constitutes a point of view which the reader can either submit to or reject. This is an approach which produces a great deal of satisfaction for the critic, who is afforded by this construction the privileged position of demystifying the worldview that is embedded within a particular narrative structure. It may, however, not be the most fruitful approach for eliciting reader identification and the affective relationship characteristic of popular literature consumption.

In a discussion of the forces which drive the relationship between a narrative and its readers, Robyn Warhol makes some relevant observations regarding women writers and readers, generally. She notes that feminist narratology distinguishes between the implied reader of a text and the actual, embodied reader because those relationships are differentiated by their affective responses to the text. The implied reader, she notes, must accept the basic assumptions that govern the narrative or she cannot "find herself effectively interpellated by narration. . . ."[27] One can conclude then that the implied reader is defined by an objective relationship to the text. On the other hand, the actual reader's relationship to the text is defined in a much more subjective manner. She, too, must accept the basic premises which determine the mode of narration but she also requires that the author adhere to a certain set of narrative expectations "to be able to take on—if only for the time of the reading—the feelings and assumptions of the implied reader: in short to be a fan."[28] The actual reader's intolerance for diversions from expected narrative features is especially pronounced in popular fiction, which tends to rely heavily on formulaic approaches.

The elaboration of these two positions sheds light on the positive reception of African American women's popular writing in spite of the lack of aesthetic sophistication bemoaned by critics. Moreover, it helps to focalize the specific kinds of authority both readers and writers brings to bear in this relationship. While Warhol draws the conclusion that the actual readers she discusses find themselves constituted as gendered subjects through these "continually reiterated affects," I want to suggest that the audiences for African American women's popular writing are not only constituted by but are constitutive of the texts. This additional function reflects the residue of African American aural aesthetics and illustrates how these texts deserve consideration alongside the canon that emerged in the late twentieth century.

When, as in the case of much black women's popular fiction, an author takes the approach of subordinating formal innovation and making the social context the explicit subject and motive of the narrative, she relinquishes some of her authorial privilege. The weight of her own perspective is necessarily diminished by the implicit invitation to the audience to confirm the success of the narrative through its affective response. This mutuality enacts the dynamics of call and response, one of the earliest mechanisms of African American narrative. The author and her text together take the lead in observing the conditions in which they exist collectively, and the audience affirms, supplements, echoes, or embellishes the accuracy of the observations through its testimonial response. The notion of testimony provides an important correlate to the notion of the embodied reader because embedded in it is the notion of emotional or affective response. Testimony in African American religious culture can in fact be mute—involving merely gestures or the expression of tears—and, thus, captures the seemingly contradictory reality of being simultaneously observable and immeasurable. Like testifying, the response of contemporary audiences takes some forms that are easily measured (like rates of purchase) and others which are more difficult to capture (such as how they relate as individuals to a text). Still, formal and informal observation repeatedly suggests that in the sphere of contemporary popular literature the text and the audience exist in a mutually constituted relationship that depends on the presentation of situations of relevant experiences in a familiar narrative form. [29]

A brief comparison of writing in the same genre across racial lines helps to illuminate the specific readings that might be generated from the communal approach described above. McMillan's *Interruption of Everything* shares a number of key features with a genre of popular (white) women's writing which emerged in the 1990s and which, in Britain, has been dubbed the "Aga-Saga" and is often designated "Domestic Romance" in the United States. This genre, according to Deborah Philips, is one which itself responds directly to a changing political climate in the transition from the consumerist Reagan-Thatcher era to the reaction against it in the Blair-Clinton era of "caring" values and in this way may be seen to highlight a concern with social context. [30] It features "a female-protagonist who is middle-class and middle-aged . . . the foregrounding of domestic life and . . . a rural setting." [31] Typically, the narrative focuses on the heroine's efforts to deal with an emotionally or financially unreliable partner, her sapped creativity and the pain of children leaving home, while simultaneously refusing to deal directly with "these vaguely defined dissatisfactions." [32] The conventional plot arc traces the heroine's dawning dissatisfaction with her husband, a flirtation with an old flame to affirm her continued sexual attractiveness, her retreat from the family and, finally, some crises which forces her "recognition of the pivotal role that a wife and mother plays within the home." [33]

In *The Interruption of Everything*, the character's familial dissatisfaction is, initially presented in terms very consistent with the genre as described above. However, as the story unfolds, the narrative reveals the complex dynamics of her race, class, and gender positioning in a way that speaks directly to the post–civil rights context. Marilyn's experience as a married, middle-class black woman mirrors that of the Aga-Saga heroine and contrasts that of the single black professional but, nonetheless, captures an important aspect of the impact of black social mobility in the post–civil rights era. As the gap between the black middle class and the black working class has grown more prominent, both public policy and popular discourses have posited the nuclear family arrangement as a potential solution to the problems of crime and economic stagnation associated with the working class and underclass. By offering an account which examines families across the class divide, exposes the constraints the nuclear family structure presents for women's autonomy, and observes the absence of structures of opportunity in working and underclass communities, the novel challenges the family restoration narrative.

It presents a narrative of middle-class black family life which initially seems to validate the aspiration to social mobility. Her children are well-educated and successful, she has been freed from necessity of working for pay (although she does have a kind of hobby job), and resides in an idyllic suburban home. Crises in her marriage and in her mother's health, though, serve to expose the hidden privileges as well as the hidden costs of such an idealized social position. As she negotiates these crises, she embarks on a journey of personal transformation and spends more time with her mother and sister in their working-class neighborhood, both of which reveal Marilyn's personal situation as a metonym for larger social dynamics.

By constructing her character's rehabilitation in relation to several working-class African American women, McMillan consciously addresses the stratification of the African American community and its impact on marriage and family, subjects which are at the forefront of black community dialogue. One prominent way in which this concern with bridging the class gap is expressed is through the characterization of the relationship between Marilyn and her drug-addicted, adopted sister Joy whose life and insights offer a counterpoint to Marilyn's own. Even the geographic dimension of their relationship echoes social developments in the post–civil rights era, with Marilyn occupying an idyllic suburb while Joy occupies the home that they'd grown up in, situated in what has become a "typical" inner city. From her home Marilyn can, for instance, "look out [her] back window . . . [and] see hundreds of acres of a green valley, the tops of which look like broccoli"[34] while Joy continues to occupy their childhood home in a Fresno neighborhood that had seen better days.

Their relationship refracts the segmentation of the African American population in the post–civil rights era. According to scholar Donna L. Franklin, by 1976 studies had already begun to indicate that "the economic impact of the civil rights movement on the poorest African-American's had been miniscule." In fact, she argues "the inequality had been greater than it had been forty years earlier."[35] Conditions have only worsened since 1976. One example of the limited impact of civil rights for some is seen in the urbanization and isolation of the poorest African Americans in ghetto communities as the few African American's who benefit from the changes wrought by the civil rights movement relocate to suburban communities.[36] However, Joy is not merely a foil for Marilyn. As she points out, they are trying to manage some of the same issues such as fear of the unknown and mustering confidence in their ability to meet the challenges they face. By linking their affective experiences, the novel creates a symbolic bridge across this gap which has come to characterize black communal relations.

Another significant change in the post–civil rights African American community has to do with the changing constitution of family, and the novel addresses this development, as well. For reasons that have to do both with an increase in incarceration among African American males as well as greater rates of educational attainment among African American women, female-headed households are increasingly common. Patricia Collins, for instance, notes that "by 1999, less than half (47 percent) of all Black families were married-couple families, 45 percent were maintained by women with no spouses."[37] There are a number of characters in the novel who typify the range of black female-headed households. The character, Joy, has already been mentioned. Additionally, the characters Orange and Blue, as well as Marilyn's friend, Bunny, help to establish a picture of the emotional and financial weight being borne by single African American women. Marilyn observes the younger women's ill-equipped efforts at parenting and the children whom they produce, who "don't stand a chance . . . don't understand grace or tenderness or pride."[38] She observes, too, their genuine desire to be good parents and sympathizes with their understanding that to do so requires "more than some damn love."[39] Implicit in the conclusion, proffered by Orange, that love is not sufficient to raising children is the necessity of financial security and emotional support. The elaborate detailing of the minutia of the sisters' diet and health, unpaid bills, relationship to parents, and romantic possibilities as well as their place in an informal economy—they braid hair together and one sells marijuana—emphasizes exactly the structures of opportunity beyond love that they lack. In spite of these characterizations, though, in her interactions with Blue and Orange as well as Joy, Marilyn is able to hear their assessments of the pitfalls of her own situation and "knows [they] are telling [her] something [she] hasn't heard."[40]

What they are telling her illuminates that middle-class motherhood and the experience of working-class mothers are often two sides of the same coin; each inextricably linked to an economy of social value. The middle-class mother acquires social value because she enacts a politics of respectability while the working-class mother is seen as a social problem not a product of the specific social forces of the moment. These characters help her to understand the political implications of marriage as a social and individual contract. She sees that her marriage has provided her with structures of opportunity that have seriously increased the potential for her to exercise personal autonomy. In this light, her failure to fully utilize those structures has a political resonance—as an individual she is wasting opportunities that others are denied as a class. In bringing these processes of valuation to the fore, the novel knits these communities together in their fictional world. Moreover, they provide a framework for understanding how Marilyn's choice to return to her marriage and to begin mothering anew through the adoption of her orphaned niece and nephew is not a mere capitulation to the ideology of female domesticity.

Because the politicization of family life has historically been overtly understood within the African American community, it is not surprising that

Marilyn's personal crises are symptoms of a larger social crisis. This novel contrasts the functioning of families across the class divide in order to suggest that in the post–civil rights era the family, and the woman's role in it, continues to be a flashpoint for understanding the social prospects of the group as a whole. So even though this novel winds up, like the Aga-Saga, affirming a domestic order, it does so not in the interest of traditional morality per se, but more in recognition of the particular social needs of African Americans in the contemporary era. Instead of confining the protagonist's contacts to her own social sphere, as is commonly the case with the domestic romance, Marilyn's relationships with women across class are crucial to her recognition of her own complicity in the demise of her personal aspirations.

The women who populate this novel reflect African American women's realities across the class spectrum and the novel's insistence on articulating these links across class offers readers a space, filled with humor and the certainty of resolution, from which to examine their own fragmented experiences. Thus, bringing these various perspectives into dialogue with each other reveals something more profound than mere celebration or indulgence of middle-class malaise. It demonstrates the same impulse toward shared experiences that defines the reading practices of "actual" audiences, for whom occupying shared ground is an essential aspect of their reading choices. Thus, when Phyllis, of the Nubian Book Club, claims of Marilyn, "She could be anyone's mother, sister, and/or friend—and that is the beauty and uncanny simplicity of it" she expresses the way in which the sense of recognition also produces an emotional response.[41]

72 HOUR HOLD: CHALLENGING THE ARCHETYPAL STRONG BLACK WOMAN

In a move that is strikingly similar to the beginning of Ansa's novel, Bebe Moore Campbell's *72 Hour Hold* also begins with an exposition that centralizes the differences between its socio-economic setting and that of previous generations. Meditating on the smoothness of her daughter's skin, the main character thinks how by contrast, hard work and the struggle for survival had marked her grandmother's skin. She awakens at her home in a middle-class African American enclave of Los Angeles, View Park: "So there I was clueless: lolling in the bed, stretching my legs and my toes—which needed a pedicure . . ." From there she moves to a description of her daughter, Trina, "still fresh from last night's bath and smell[ing] like Dove and that pale yellow lotion in the big plastic bottle."[42] The affluence implied by the lolling and the pedicure, along with the invocation of specific consumer products, work to locate both the character and the text in the late twentieth century. This specificity is reinforced by the contrast with the past when Keri thinks how that lotion would not have been sufficient to the task of her grandmother's feet because "when you grow up plowing Georgia clay barefoot in the hard time, nothing on or in you remains soft."[43] Here Campbell contrasts the two eras and establishes the idea that certain models of femininity can be incompatible with specific historical moments. Thus she primes the reader to begin to reconsider the value of the archetype of the strong black woman from the perspective of how it impacts the woman as individual.

While ultimately this novel will focus on this mother's struggle to provide adequate care for her daughter who suffers from bi-polar disorder, it also accounts for her own emotional vulnerability as a single black woman. The questions with which Keri struggles—to determine how much of herself to sacrifice for others, how not to experience her daughter's illness as a sign of her failure as a mother, and how to accept the help that is offered to her by others—are all questions which serve to exemplify the heightened tension between the "freedom" of the post–civil rights black subject and the continuing impact of "controlling images" such as the strong black woman, derived from the eras of slavery and Jim Crow. In this way, Campbell's text exposes another dangerous dimension of black female success, thus expanding public interrogation of the way in which the strong black woman stereotype operates in contemporary culture. In her essay, "Patricia Hill Collins's *Black Sexual Politics* and the Genealogy of the Strong Black Woman," critic Jean Wyatt helps to illuminate the way in which the "denigrating messages" embodied in the stereotype continue to be perpetuated, "unacknowledged, in their more subtle contemporary embodiments."[44]

In this essay, Wyatt provides an analysis of the stereotype's function in the era of slavery, the mid-twentieth century, and in the post–civil rights era. In the first two eras the ways in which the stereotype served the maintenance of a white power structure is fairly obvious; the notion of the strong black woman justified a slew of atrocities committed on her under slavery and its iteration as the Black Matriarch could be used to deflect attention away from inequitable political and economic systems in the 1960s. By the turning of the twenty-first century, however, its operation is more subtle because the nature of racial oppression has changed and because black women are themselves embracing and perpetuating the stereotype.[45] However, Wyatt's examination of texts by Collins as well as post-soul generation critics Veronica Chambers and Joan Morgan, exposes the degree to which "internalizing the image [of the strong black woman] as one's own gender identity must continue to serve the interests of racist ideology and so perpetuate one's own oppression" because that image originates in discourses of oppressive racial justification.[46] Regardless of the degree to which individual women do or do not recognize the damage done by the Strong Black Woman syndrome, it is certainly not an issue that is seen as central to the conversation on continued black social progress.

In light of the absence of discussion around this phenomenon, Campbell's stages an important engagement of the subjective traumas of post–civil rights black womanhood. Whereas the other texts examined in this chapter intervene in discourses with at least some recognition in the public sphere, the issue of black female emotional health has not gained traction in the way that the "epidemic" of singleness or the restoration of the nuclear family as palliative to social and economic crises have; in this regard it may be the text in which the goal of responding to a social crises rather than an aesthetic criteria is most pronounced. Indeed, of the three texts examined herein, this one deals most directly with emotional pain as a social issue which pervades contemporary black women's experience.

Though Campbell clearly intended to de-stigmatize mental illness in the African American community, her use of this topic can also be seen to function metaphorically to indicate other unacknowledged disease in the community. For instance, the impact of the Strong Black Woman syndrome is brought to the fore in a way that allows the reader to recognize this crisis in her own life and to bring her own experiences to bear on the text in a way that allows for a mutual articulation of the post–civil rights experience. Central to the engagement of that experience in this text is the juxtaposition of Keri's middle-class "freedom" with her bondage to her role as a good mother.

This sense of self is reflected in both her personal and professional lives. At work, in her high-end resale clothing store she has assembled a group of women for whom she is the nurturer and stabilizing force. Her role as nurturer, in fact, often overshadows her role as a successful Los Angeles entrepreneur. For example, her employees include a former call girl, Adriana, "who wasn't the only redeemed soul working with [Keri]" since, "Right before [Keri] hired her, Frances had lived in a shelter for battered women."[47] Even though Keri's narration suggests that the three have come together for a reason, she seems not to realize that her choosing them as employees stems from her immense sense of responsibility to others over herself. Certainly, from a strictly business perspective, these women would not seem to be the most rational choices for employees, given the inherent instability of their lives when she hires them.

Though she feels obliged to extend help to others in need, Keri, ironically, is marked by her inability to accept the help that is offered her. In particular she rejects the help offered by her mother, Emma, a recovering addict. Although Emma has successfully rebuilt her life, Keri rejects Emma's help because she still suffers from the wounds inflicted by Emma's binge drinking and abandonment of Keri to her grandmother's care, when Keri was a child. Tellingly, in response to one counselor's advice that she focus on Trina's capacity for healing, she begins to think of her mother: "But you left me home alone when I was three. You didn't come to my open house at school when I was five, six, seven, eight, nine. You threw up all over my prom gown. You were drunk at my graduation. You didn't show up at my wedding. You didn't come when the baby died."[48] Her response articulates the similarity of her need for healing and her daughter's but she will not allow herself to recognize it.

Instead of considering the fact that her daughter's brain disease parallels her own heart-sickness, she responds by going for a run, redirecting the source of the pain she feels from the mental to the physical. Of the physical pain she thinks: "that kind of pain . . . didn't cause me to mourn a man, a marriage, and a child," and, so, she is able to continue to push herself forward in a way that she might not be able to if she forced herself to examine her own emotions.[49] In deflecting attention from her personal pain and vulnerability, she remains bound to the sense of herself as a strong woman able to handle any of the external obstacles confronted by contemporary women.

Keri's inability to let go of the middle-class horizon of expectation she had for her daughter is another example of how she refuses to recognize the toll of the standards she sets for herself. Though she can recognize and even argue to her ex-husband that Trina's illness, like any other, is beyond their control and must be acknowledged and treated as such, she still cannot help but see its interruption of Trina's social development as a marker of personal failure. While ensconced in one of the safe-houses operated by the guerrilla treatment group she seeks out as a last desperate measure to avoid institutionalizing Trina, she watches the apparent serenity of one of the group members (the parent of a mentally ill child herself) and thinks, "maybe she never really expected much out of life . . . maybe that's why she can be content with her sunflowers and her boy who will never be the same."[50] Though she knows, logically, the impossibility of it she continues to pursue a full recovery for Trina because, as one of the doctors puts it, she thinks "[her] daughter's bipolar disorder is [her] personal tragedy" and "want[s] the bright child back, who attends Brown and gets straight A's."[51] Pointedly Keri rejects the advice she gets from members of the group to accept her daughter's limitations, resenting their telling her what to want for either her daughter or herself.[52]

While of course these would be understandable and natural reactions for any parent, as is common for most black people, Keri's perceptions are filtered through a lens of awareness of historical racial attitudes. At one point, for instance, she wonders if the team's approach to treating Trina reflects any racial bias: "If Trina had been a little blond girl, would they have presumed compliance and passivity, been less on guard, treated her more kindly? If I'd been a white woman with a husband, would it have made a difference in what they expected?"[53] The irony of course is that Keri can see the ways in which racial attitudes might affect the treatment and perception of her daughter, but is not aware of how the same might impact her self-perception. Campbell however cannot be accused of the same lack of awareness; in her use of the trope of an escaping slave to explicate Keri's "run for freedom" we see her insistence that readers recognize this strong black woman's struggle as rooted in a bygone era.

Again and again Campbell has Keri elucidating her experience through metaphors drawn from the experiences of African American slaves. For example, in order to describe the fruitlessness of foreknowledge when dealing with the onset of psychotic symptoms in her daughter she thinks "And what difference would it have made anyhow? Knowing that the hounds are tracking you doesn't mean you won't get caught; it means you have to get to the swamp fast."[54] Elsewhere, the periods in which Trina is committed to care and returned to home are, respectively, likened to a child torn from a mother's arms on "a Charleston auction block" and her return is figured in terms of "Massa ha[ving] changed his mind, brought back the slave child, and placed her in her mother's arms along with manumission papers for both."[55] The choice of this governing metaphor is one that assumes a shared point of reference with an audience composed primarily of black women, for whom slavery's assault on maternity would be likely to elicit a strong affective response. Throughout the narration, these images of bondage are contrasted with Keri's relative affluence and the horizon of her expectations for her daughter—the supposed markers of the post–civil rights generation. Keri's run is, in fact, presented as an extension of the historical effort of black women to access what they need and speaks to others who may be trying to reconcile their own contradictory experiences of social freedom and emotional bondage.

Throughout, Campbell draws a parallel with the historical experience of slavery using the trope of slavery not just to describe the bondage in which the families of the mentally ill exist or the psychic pressure that African American women must face as the primary heads of families, but also to suggest the degree to which the silence around the issue of black women's vulnerability limits our freedom as a community. In this way, like the authors I have previously examined, Campbell demonstrates an awareness of the need to examine complex aspects of black experience which are not captured by a black/white dichotomy. Instead, they reflect a commitment to creating "novels that speak to the diversity of our experiences" within the group.[56]

CONCLUSION

The social context of the post–civil rights era has created numerous changes in the popular cultural market place. As with other spheres of culture such as music, film and television, and athletic entertainment, black literary professionals have attained a significant, if not dominant presence. One result of this increased production of black-themed or black-populated cultural material is a more demanding and segmented audience. The proliferation of a variety of black entertainments affords audiences a level of selectivity unimagined when the publication of literature by and about black people was an infrequent occurrence. This means to a large extent we can rely on the choices of these audiences to provide reliable information regarding their self-perception, social attitudes, and sources of pleasure. In a time when African American women have had unprecedented access to professional employment at the same time that they have been least likely to marry, more likely to shoulder the economic and emotional responsibilities of African American family life, mass fiction that take on themes of personal fulfillment and success in personal relationships strike a chord with consumers. These works document and publicize the social reality of African American women's roles as heads of their households, the economic and emotional centers of the black family as well as the economic vulnerability of such households and the likelihood that such women will continue to face these struggles alone. Critics who are concerned with the fate of black literature and black people need to recognize how certain constructions of literariness—rooted in the ideology of Western formal literacy and the author as sole maker of meaning—may in fact be excluding us from some important conversations regarding African American women. Conversely, by taking these texts into consideration, s/he may gain valuable insights into the ways in which contemporary African American women writers and readers grounded in more communal narrative practices, extend concepts of blackness to include both gender and class as prominent aspects of black subjectivity.

NOTES

1. Jaqueline Bobo, *Black Women as Cultural Readers*, (New York: Columbia University Press, 1995), 5.
2. Harris-Perry, *Sister Citizen*, 96.
3. Hooks, *Communion*, 52.
4. Bobo, *Black Women*, 5.
5. I am using the term mass fiction to denote a combination of high sales and visible positioning in physical book stores, the presence of a set of narrative characteristics which include a tendency to be formulaic and to address the experiences of an identifiable subculture in a way that reflects rather than challenges its experiences, and being understood by the audience as objects of consumption rather than tools of discovery. This definition draws on Mary Rogers's discussion of the "common reader" in her study, *Novels, Novelists, and Readers: Toward a Phenomenological Sociology of Literature*.
6. Herman Gray, *Cultural Moves*, 16.
7. Henry Louis Gates, *The Signifying Monkey*, 49.
8. Ibid., 50.
9. Gray, *Moves*, 13.
10. Bobo, *Black Women*, 16.
11. Tina Ansa, *The Hand I Fan With*, 19.

12. Donna Franklin. *Ensuring Inequality, The Structural Transformation of the African-American Family* (New York: Oxford University Press, 1997), 219.

13. It should be stated that all of the texts examined depict primarily heterosexual social worlds and so my arguments basically respond to that construction. This is not meant to presume that all post–civil rights African American women are heterosexual nor that this omission in the literature should not be critiqued. Such critique is, however, beyond the purview of this work.

14. Ansa, *Hand*, 110.

15. Donna Franklin, *What's Love Got to Do With It? Understanding and Healing the Rift Between Black Men and Women* (New York: Simon & Schuster, 2000), 66.

16. Ansa, *Hand*, 89.

17. Ibid., 214.

18. Ibid., 213.

19. Ibid., 108.

20. Ibid., 213.

21. Ibid., 108.

22. Franklin, *Love*, 165.

23. Ansa, *Hand*, 225.

24. Ibid., 472.

25. Paulette Richards, *Terry McMillan: A Critical Companion* (Westport, Connecticut: Greenwood Press, 1999), 17.

26. Bobo, *Black Women*, 51–52.

27. Robyn Warhol, 145.

28. Ibid., 148.

29. I have already cited, in various sections of this work, the formal observations of Jacqueline Bobo, Lawrence Levine, Mary Rogers, and Robyn Warhol. To these and my own informal observations of testimonial at book club conferences and author websites, we could also add the work of Janice Radway.

30. Deborah Phillips, *Women's Fiction 1945–2005: Writing Romance* (London: Continuum Books, 2006), 96.

31. Ibid., 97.

32. Ibid., 100–102.

33. Ibid., 101.

34. Terry McMillan, *The Interruption of Everything*, (New York: Signet Books, 2006), 169.

35. Franklin, *Ensuring*, 187.

36. Franklin, *Ensuring*, 189.

37. Collins, 80.

38. McMillan, *Interruption*, 144.

39. Ibid., 343.

40. Ibid., 259.

41. "Middle-Age Melodrama." Amazon.com: Customer Reviews: The Interruption of Everything. http://www.amazon.com/The-Interruption-Everything-Terry-McMillan/dp/B000B LNPGY. September 19, 2014.

42. Bebe Moore Campbell, *72 Hour Hold* (New York: Anchor Books, 2006), 4.

43. Campbell, *Hold*, 4.

44. Jean Wyatt, "Patricia Hill Collin's *Black Sexual Politics* and the Genealogy of the Strong Black Woman," *Studies in Gender and Sexuality* 9, no.1 (2008): 61.

45. Ibid., 58.

46. Ibid., 61–62.

47. Campbell, *Hold*, 66.

48. Ibid., 205.

49. Ibid., 206.

50. Ibid., 207.

51. Ibid., 217.

52. Ibid., 202.

53. Ibid., 188.

54. Ibid., 3.
55. Ibid., 28, 33.
56. Ibid., 181.

Chapter Four

Feminism and the Streets

Urban Fiction and the Quest for Female
Independence in the Era of Transactional Sexuality

with David Ikard

The preceding chapters have suggested that African American popular literature engages multiple segments of the black public sphere. This chapter turns
to urban fiction's engagement of feminist discourses. The dialog established
in these texts offers challenges to academic feminism and widens the conversation on black sexual politics. Such an examination of black sexuality is
crucial to black publicity because it has been a primary way in which black
bodies have been legislated in the post–civil rights era. As Patricia Hill
Collins points out in the introduction to *Black Sexual Politics*, issues such as
HIV/AIDS, adolescent pregnancy, and children as dependents of the state are
all issues which intersect with anti-racist activism. Thus, the themes that are
identified in this chapter shed light on the ways in which popular fiction
functions as a platform for black female interventions in the black public
sphere.

In urban fiction, we can see an example of literature's function as part of
a black counter-public. Through its thematic reach and affective frame it
makes important contributions to our understanding of discursive constructions of black communal gender politics. Urban fiction can be understood as
an important segment of black public discourse in part through its mechanisms of production, in which the mode of self-publication figures prominently. In the context of self-publishing, many black women have found an
opportunity to connect with conversations on black sexuality and black family structures which, in the twenty-first century, more commonly circulate via
Internet and televisual media.

While not all urban fiction is self-published, the trend toward self-publication in this genre is strong enough to warrant some discussion here. Vickie Stringer's experience provides an example. Her first novel, *Let That Be the Reason*, presented a serious challenge to the corporate publishing industry which initially shunned it and others like it as too violent, to sexually graphic, and lacking the polish and refinement of prose that would allow readers to take these publications seriously. However, Stringer, among others, recognized the degree to which a segment of readers would take to the books specifically because of these characteristics. In spite of numerous rejections from mainstream publishing houses Stringer maintained her belief that her novel would sell because it "was hip hop." Finally in 2002 she decided to establish Triple Crown Publications, named after the drug selling organization with which she had been involved, and publish and distribute her own novel. The novel proved immensely popular and soon other street lit authors were submitting their work to her and within a few years Triple Crown was publishing up to twenty-five novels a year. Subsequently, numerous independent publishers of urban fiction such as Life Changing Books and Deja King Productions, have emerged as well as urban fiction imprints associated with larger corporate publishing houses such as Simon and Schuster, Little Brown, and Ballantine's, and many titles are available formatted for Kindle.

The success of figures like Vickie Stringer and Triple Crown Publications can be measured in more than financial terms. The freedom offered by self-publication enables the development of new approaches to traditional themes in African American literature. For instance, urban fiction has drawn on the aesthetics of hip hop musical culture to address the subject of economic mobility. The genre both records and challenges the false divide between hustlin' and mainstream legitimacy. In its narratives it presents us with a panoply of characters pursuing the American Dream—in a perversion of Malcolm X's oft-quoted slogan—by any means necessary. This ethos is intimately tied to the terms of production which enabled the rise of urban fiction.

New territories opened up by urban fiction go beyond troubling the line between legitimate and illegitimate economic pursuits. The conversations it has engendered regarding the intersection of race and sexuality are most important for our inquiries here. Indeed, in relationship to the black public sphere, it could be argued that urban fiction's most significant impact has been in the area of sexuality. The success of the genre has affected an important discursive shift in the conversation on black sexual politics by breaking through the constraints imposed by the politics of respectability which govern conversations that take place in other media spheres. The freedom to address unruly desires and the contradictions of post–civil rights social experience enables us to locate those aspects of shared reality which cement the concerns of various members of the African American community, however they are positioned via generational affiliation or class.

In addition to highlighting issues of shared concern, the emphasis on structures of feeling over formal sophistication is another important way in which urban fiction can function to create bonds among various African American female publics. In her analysis of hip hop fiction by women, Eve Dunbar offers the idea of non-liberatory agency as a concept that might help us to make sense of the contradictions that exist within women's hip hop fiction. This concept, she argues, offers an alternative to total liberation and recognizes the value of black women's efforts to "find space to create and tell their stories through embodying the very forms that seek to oppress them."[1] Keying in on a concept like non-liberatory agency helps us to understand the affective power of such texts by registering female assertions of power that do not conform to conventional feminist measures. By mirroring black women's struggle to shape their own lives in a context in which most social forces work to disempower them on the basis of race and gender, urban fiction's presentation of non-liberatory agency opens the possibility for reader identification.

Though gender relations in hip hop culture are a hotly debated topic they rarely focus on female agency. Instead, critiques of misogyny in commercial rap music typically dominate. Charges of hyper-masculinity and female objectification fly, while conservative popular discourse indicts the culture as pathological and defenders view hip hop as authentic expressions of racial and economic disaffection. Because the popular debate tends to get bogged down in either defensive or critical positions it rarely explores the nuances and complexities of the negotiations of gender ideology that take place in hip hop cultural expression. This does not mean, however, that hip hop storytelling has no impact on the politics of gender. Rather, it is the limiting of our understanding of hip hop culture to merely the rap narratives that prevents the recognition of the complex negotiations of gender ideology that are at the center of the post–civil rights, hip hop era popular cultural landscape.

In this chapter we examine urban fiction as a literary genre rooted in the storytelling aesthetic of hip hop culture, to assess its contributions to the popular discourse on gender. We argue that its engagement of archetypes of female empowerment such as the "Bitch," the desire for romantic coupling, and the struggle for control of female reproduction are continuous with black feminist efforts to theorize gender experience in the post–civil rights era. Specifically, we understand these texts to do the following: 1) extend the concern of traditional feminist theorizing with the quest for female independence; 2) engage the contradictions of feminist theory and practice engendered by individual sexual desire articulated by hip hop feminists; and 3) offer provocative representations of black men, which correlate with black male feminism's concern with examining family structures and challenging the reproduction of rigid definitions of black masculinity.

While it may seem counterintuitive to turn to such an excoriated genre as urban fiction to begin an assessment of feminism in the black community, its roots in hip hop culture help to explain why one might do so. The emergence of hip hop culture has been associated with a very distinct generational experience. As Tricia Rose remarks, hip hop is the first black musical form to be associated with a collective, generational lifestyle and experience.[2] In turn critics have enumerated hip hop culture's impacts on political awareness and participation, the mobilization of new constructions of identity, and feminist theorizing among that generation. Patricia Hill Collins takes up the latter in *From Black Power to Hip Hop,* identifying the unique relationship of hip hop generation women of color to feminism. She argues that this relationship is mediated by their need to "carve out a space that simultaneously accepts and rejects the tenets of feminism and nationalism."[3] This attempt to carve out such a space has necessitated a move away from traditional academic approaches. Hill Collins reads the surge in the publication of personal narratives by women of color in the 1990s as an important development for engaging the complicated relationship of the hip hop generation to feminism. In moving away from "scholarly venues and other traditional outlets for feminist thought," hip hop generation feminists respond to the increased salience of the popular cultural sphere in the post–civil rights era.[4] Hill Collins argues that this shift of feminist theorizing into the popular cultural sphere may in fact constitute a new mobilization of the feminist movement, which she sees as having been in abeyance since the 1980s.

Joan Morgan's *When Chickenheads Come Home to Roost* is, possibly, the ur-text of hip hop feminism. Award-winning journalist and lover of hip hop, Morgan's style of feminism attends to the sometimes competing impulses of racial solidarity and gender equity in a "real talk" style that resonates with the hip hop generation. Consider some of the provocative questions she raises:

Can you be a good feminist and admit out loud that there are things you kind of dig about patriarchy?

Is it foul to say that imagining a world where you could paint your big brown lips in the most decadent of shades, pile your phat ass into your fave micromini, slip your freshly manicured toes (sic) into four-inch fuck me sandals and have not one single solitary man objectify—I mean roam his eyes longingly over all the intended place—is, like, a total drag for you?

Are we no longer good feminists, not to mention nineties supersistas, if the A.M.'s wee hours sometimes leave us tearful and frightened that achieving all our mothers wanted us to—great educations, careers, financial and emotional independence—has made us wholly undesirable to the men who are supposed to be our counterparts? Men whose fascination with chickenheads leaves us convinced they have no interest in dating let alone marrying, their equals?[5]

Such questions direct our attention to the "complexity inherent in being black girls now—sistas of the post–Civil Rights, post-feminist, post-soul, hip-hop generation."[6] The "phat" ass floating above those four-inch heels, in Morgan's characterization, is enlivened in ways that academic feminism's more abstract formulations of "female sexual desire" may never be. Additionally, the emphasis on "good feminists" in these questions points to the traditionally proscriptive nature of academic feminism (or at least many people's experiences of it).

A distinct feature of the hip hop aesthetic, captured in Morgan's text and other hip hop inflected materials, is a use of direct language that captures lexical meaning as well as felt meaning. This is, in part, a reflection of a distinctly black approach to the word.[7] It is also linked to the urgency of the situation out of which hip hop culture emerged. The social context of the post-industrial, post–civil rights era with its racialized attacks on black communities created the need for a discourse which made the obscure transparent. In its initial stages and during the Golden Age of the early to middle nineties, hip hop articulated the impact of public policies which were not specifically racial but nonetheless had the most significant impacts among urban blacks and Latinos.[8] Hip hop success in this era was based largely on its ability to affirm the lived experience of these citizens and to make it transparent to others.

Though the contemporary context is in some ways different, hip hop culture still reflects this ethos of rendering the social dynamics of power visible. As the forms of hip hop culture and other aspects of American culture have become increasingly commodified, hip hop's primary tropes have shifted to reflect a preoccupation with commercial forms of power. The emergence of the pimp/ho discourse is a significant marker of this preoccupation. It simultaneously refracts the commodification of race and social relations and frames the dynamics of heterosexual romance via the trope of transactional sexuality. The emphasis on this kind of exchange has been vigorously and rightfully critiqued for its misogyny. However, coming fully to terms with the complexity of transactional sexuality in contemporary hip hop culture is no simple matter.

T. Denean Sharpley-Whiting's analysis of black gender relations in the hip hop era, *Pimps Up, Ho's Down*, is particularly useful for fleshing out these complications. That she grounds her analysis of standards of beauty in video culture, strip club culture, groupie culture, and discursive responses to sexual violence against black women in the trope of "pimpin" is suggestive because each category is linked to larger processes of exchange that exceed those between individual men and women. Sharpley-Whiting offers the provocative idea that the commercial success of hip hop culture (typically characterized as a male-dominated form) is heavily dependent upon the presence of young black women. She explains: "Overexposed young black female flesh 'pimpin',' 'playin',' and 'checkin' in videos, television, film, rap lyrics, fashion, and on the Internet, is indispensable to the mass-media-engineered appeal of hip hop culture, which is helping to shape a new black gender politics."[9] In drawing our attention to media conglomerations as part of hip hop's pimp/ho nexus, Sharpley-Whiting begins to expose the centrality of transactional sexuality to American culture. She links the preference for "ascriptive mulattas" (those who have the characteristic of light skin and wavy hair texture of the racially "mixed" person, whether they are mixed or not) and the "exotic" Latina in music and pornographic video culture to transactional sexuality. She further traces media participation in the trading of black female sexuality for dollars in strip club cultures, which have not only "gone mainstream," but have become central to the business of hip hop. The strip club has taken on "a male boardroom atmosphere where deals are brokered, video vixens are scouted, invitations [among rappers] to appear on records are extended, and records are broken [debuted] . . ."[10] As part of her larger goal of describing how black women negotiate gender and sexuality within these constraints, she also examines the phenomenon of hip hop groupies and the power dynamics that inform their attempts to bed famous hip hop stars as well as their efforts to parlay those experiences into dollars in the form of "tell-all" book publications. Ultimately, "In these scenarios, sex simultaneously becomes one way to exert some semblance of control and power in relationships . . ."[11]

Given that this transactional approach to black female sexuality is rooted in a longer history of commodifying black women's bodies, it should come as no surprise that black women's literature has a deep history of engaging this political reality. Zora Neale Hurston's, *Their Eyes Were Watching God* exemplifies such a critical engagement. This text is universally understood as a critique of marriage as an institution in which female bodies are exchanged for social capital and is celebrated because of Janie's apparent ability to find independence in spite of these norms. The force of Hurston's critique rests on the fact that in her social context the asymmetrical relationships of power that informed these exchanges between men and women were obscured by gender ideologies that naturalized them.

Similarly, urban fiction examines the complications that arise when women pursue sexual relationships and personal fulfillment in a context in which relations of power are more explicit rendered and gender roles are, presumably, more fluid. Interestingly, in the debates regarding urban fiction, *Their Eyes Were Watching God* has shown up repeatedly as a benchmark of black literary endeavor. Various commentaries, focusing on its themes of sexuality and black language usage, have alternatively used it to justify urban fiction as a literary endeavor or to demonstrate its failure as such. In an essay in which she argues that urban fiction (or "street" fiction, as she calls it) can coexist with more traditional forms of black literature, Danyel Smith concludes by citing a passage from Hurston's text, in which the narrative details a highly sexualized vision of Janie as she returns to town. The cited passage also includes a conversation about the (in)appropriateness of Janie's relationship with Tea Cake. Smith's essay is, in part, a response to Nick Chiles's January 4, 2006 *New York Times* editorial "Their Eyes Were Reading Smut." In this editorial he bemoans the commercial displacement of traditional "African American Literature" by street lit, which he deems nothing more than "pornography for black women."[12]

Though Chiles does not make direct comparison with *Their Eyes Were Watching God*, his title is clearly intended to suggest the distance between the content and concerns of canonical black literature and those of urban fiction. Maintaining this perception, however, requires that the reader ignore exactly what Smith's quote highlights—that Hurston's text centralizes sexual imagery and the celebration of sexual pleasure in ways that are quite similar to contemporary urban fiction. Attending to the similarities among these texts, on the other hand, helps to illuminate urban fiction's place in a continuum of black feminist theorizing. As Patricia Hill Collins reminds us, African American women's literature has historically functioned as "a legitimate voice for African American women's [political] thought."[13] We understand urban fiction to participate in this political project by engaging the lived experience of black womanhood in the context of transactional sexuality.

As noted earlier, members of the hip hop generation are constituted by their unique social locations and aesthetics. Their genesis in the post–civil rights era is a crucial factor in the engagement of complex, contradictory notions of race and gender. Civil rights era reform means that the experience of what it means to be black, for instance, has fractured so that we are required to name specific black identities and their sometimes, competing, agendas. Along the axis of gender, there is a similar need to specify class location, sexual identification, and ideological positioning, all of which play a role in framing gender experience across racial categories. Consequently, the attempt to understand contemporary black experiences must look to a wide variety of sources, including materials like urban fiction, which may, initially, seem offensive or counterproductive to progressive ideology.

THE GENERATIONAL DIVIDE AND THE ARCHETYPE OF THE BITCH

In particular, urban fiction helps us to think about the intersection of hip hop-inflected, market notions of blackness and black working-class aspiration. In this way, the genre is useful for revealing various contours of black female experience under the new black gender politics. Urban fiction's primary archetype, the Bitch, for example, is distinguished from a more traditional

literary model of black femininity. The traditional black female literary figure has been associated with the rehabilitation of black culture as a whole. As
Jacqueline Bobo rightly notes, traditionally, black women literary and visual
artists seek "to eradicate the harmful and pervasive images haunting their
history" in order to provide a "correct" interpretation of black culture.[14] A
singular, corrective image of black women is impossible in an era characterized by multiple black identities. Thus, the Bitch archetype becomes a useful
mechanism for extending the exploration of black women's sexual and political experiences without the constraining need to produce "positive" images.

Tina Ansa's 2003 novel *You Know Better* illustrates these varying generational approaches to the performance of black womanhood. One of the characters explicitly rejects the model of femininity presented by her mother's
civil rights generation. She thinks:

> It's the truth, though, about those overachieving older black women. Personal-
> ly, I don't have the energy. I don't have the time. And I don't have the
> inclination to be one of those can-do-it-all black women like my mother. They
> just don't make 'em like that anymore . . . thank God! I don't want the job. "If
> called, I will not run. If elected, I will not serve."[15]

The rejection of a "can-do-it-all" model of black femininity indicates a
rift in class and generational interests among black women. Similarly, in
demonstrating their preference for urban fiction, a segment of contemporary
African American women readers push back against other narratives of black
female experience, helping us to see how young, poor, African American
women might see themselves and their experience in relation to other African
American experiences. This resistance among readers mirrors the theoretical
shift noted earlier in which traditional academic feminist approaches are
eschewed in favor of models which capture more of the realities of hip hop
generation femininity. Urban fiction stages its entry into the literary conversation on the black woman's quest for independence in ways that are consistent with the changing norms of femininity in this era. In doing so, it registers
the slippage between feminist ideals and the contradictions of lived experience that hip hop feminism has placed at center stage.

Where the popular fiction associated with middle-class consumers and
producers is primarily concerned with the question of how individual black
women strike a balance between obligations to self and others, urban fiction
is rooted in a much more individualistic ethos. Reflecting the transactionalist
ethic of the post–civil rights era, it questions the very notion of obligations to
anyone other than self. This ethos is epitomized in one seminal urban fiction
text's refrain, "game is to be sold, not told."[16] This phrase which emerges
from the subculture of drug-dealing, conveys the sensibility that whatever
knowledge one possesses about surviving and prospering is a commodity

which should be used to further one's own goals rather than shared. The assumption that everything from "game" (specialized forms of wisdom) to female sexuality can be exchanged for more access to power is embodied in the figure of the Bitch.

The Bitch archetype popularized in urban fiction has clear roots in the quasi-feminist discourse of hip hop's "Sista With Attitude." Cheryl Keyes uses this term to describe the discursive position of female rappers of the late 1980s to the mid-1990s, who foreground an aggressive or assertive stance and attempt to reclaim the word "bitch" and link it to a subversion of patriarchal rule.[17] As it is frequently expressed in narratives that "brag about partying and smoking 'blunts' (marijuana) with their men; seducing, repressing, and sexually emasculating male characters; or 'dissin' (verbally downplaying) their would-be female or male competitors," this position is not necessarily feminist.[18] It is in fact rather fraught with contradiction as it simply follows the model of power articulated in the male gangster hero. Sharpley-Whiting identifies a similar adoption of masculine prerogative among strippers whom she characterizes as "practitioners of a swaggering black female masculinity" and "the 'new niggaz.'"[19] Like Keyes, Sharpley-Whiting exposes the limits of such masculinist strategies suggesting that they are the product of "rummaging around a junkyard of race and gender stereotypes."[20] As these stereotypes rely on the association of power and agency with masculinity and reproduce the association of passive objectification with femininity, employing them can only produce a highly qualified form of power for the women who adopt this strategy.

One of the earliest successes of the urban fiction genre, Vickie Stringer's, *Let That Be the Reason*, highlights the contradictions inherent in the deployment of the Bitch archetype. The novel's protagonist Pammy, recognizes that she must adopt a very specific, masculinized, gender position and thus develops an alter ego, Carmen, in order to realize her ambitions. According to the narrative, Pammy was "weak, emotional, and trusting." In stark contrast, Carmen was "strong, emotionless, untrusting."[21] In short, she is the prototypical Bitch.

Let That Be the Reason tells a story that is common in urban fiction by women. Its protagonist is on a quest for financial independence and must overcome several obstacles to achieve it. In this instance the character has been accustomed to a high standard of living, financed by her drug-dealing boyfriend. However, it is the boyfriend's betrayal and abandonment of her that motivate the plot. She has been left with a child whom the boyfriend, Chino, refuses to acknowledge or support. Additionally, she is unwilling to give up the standard of living to which she had become accustomed, and she turns to prostitution, which seems to offer her the rate of pay that her lifestyle requires as well as the flexibility of working hours that having a small child requires. Through these circumstances, the character develops a strong value for independence, which ultimately leads her to enter into the more profitable arena of drug sales.

Whether it takes the form of sex for money, social status, or access to information or goods, the reality of sexual trade is a standard in the genre of urban fiction. In a discussion of Deja King's novel *Bitch*, co-authors, Elizabeth Marshall, Jeanine Staples, and Simone Gibson, note that although the protagonist enacts a variety of bitchy black femininities, each is, "tied to a relationship with a man who is financially prosperous, physically attractive, and socially deviant."[22] Stringer's character, Pam/Carmen, deviates from this pattern. After her brief tenure as a prostitute, she is rather staunch in her refusal to engage in transactional sexual relationships. She understands that these kinds of relationships are not consistent with her quest for independence. Pam/Carmen's refusal to submit to the social compulsion for women to "use what they have to get what they want" distinguishes her trajectory from those of other urban fiction characters.[23] For example, Pam/Carmen's story ends with her arrest and conviction, while *Bitch*'s protagonist, Precious, "ends up the legal wife of a famous, rich rap star."[24] The distinction of these two endings foregrounds the dangers associated with the attempt to use stereotypes strategically. One either winds up reproducing the same dynamics she was trying to escape or she produces a, perhaps, too real threat to the power structure and draws its defenses. Thus, Precious is allowed to succeed because her strategy of transactional bitchiness actually reproduces the status quo of objectified female sexuality. In contrast, Pam/Carmen's more challenging iteration of the Bitch, which refuses to continue to subject her sexuality to commodification, raises the ire or suspicion of almost every male she encounters until, finally, one of them betrays her to the police.

One passage pointedly illustrates how the boundaries of masculine privilege are policed when women try to appropriate male power. After a fellow drug dealer confronts her with a question about why she doesn't have a male companion, wondering if she "can't keep one" or if "another kitty" is her preference, she responds that she was not interested in women or any man who did not meet her standards, so she was "paying" herself. The exchange continues: "Since I was holding my own, all he could do was some foul shit. He stepped to the side of my Jeep, unzipped his pants, pulled out his dick and started to pee, saying shit like 'Can you do this? Can you write your name with your dick?'" Finally he aims his stream at her feet and lands at least one drop of urine on her shoe before she is able to side step him completely, ending with the challenging call "Your turn."[25] She responds to this by calmly reiterating the idea that her power resides not with the penis but in her lack of dependence on a penis. Further emphasizing the fact that she is "paid," she removes her shoes, throws them away, and replaces them with an extra pair from her car, telling him: "It's okay, baby. I only wear my shoes one time anyway."[26]

In the final analysis, however, the efficacy of the Bitch strategy is undermined by its failure to shift dominant configurations of gender. The association of power with masculinity continues and women can only access it through coupling with a male or by acting as a male. Thus, the archetype works to reify the trope of male power, figured in terms of active consumption of passive female, instead of disrupting the dynamic of transactional sexuality.

BEYOND THE BITCH: THE RETURN OF THE COUPLING CONVENTION

Whereas Stringer's novel is a somewhat didactic engagement of the value of female independence, other novels take that value as a given and then attempt to imagine ways in which that independence can coexist in partnership with men. In doing so, they move away from the archetype of the Bitch, which is, incompatible with conventionally middle-class conceptions of success. The Bitch is associated with a very specific "ghettocentric" notion of success rooted in a normative drug/gangsta culture that is not uniformly adopted throughout urban fiction. For instance, Wahida Clark's "Thug" series, which begins with the 2005 publication of *Thugs and the Women Who Love Them*, features a set of characters—Angel, Jaz, Kyra, and Roz—who have strongly articulated educational goals and aspirations for careers in the "legitimate" world. Angel is an aspiring lawyer, Jaz a chemist, Roz a physical therapist, and Kyra a psychologist. The novels celebrate these aspirations and their collective determination "not to let the ghetto take them out."[27] For these characters, not being taken out means achieving successful, long-term coupling in addition to launching professional careers. This emphasis on romantic success is in contrast to the typical Bitch narrative, wherein sexual encounters tend to be a way to "manipulate powerful, influential men to obtain certain possessions and social positions."[28] In centralizing marriage as part and parcel of female success these novels simultaneously reanimate familiar tropes of black women's writing and expose the inconsistencies which undermine women's efforts to achieve independence in the era of transactional sexuality.

In *The Coupling Convention*, Ann duCille traces the use of the marriage plot in literature by African American women from the mid-nineteenth to mid-twentieth centuries. She identifies marriage as a trope which has functioned politically, figuring the racial quest for freedom as well as the individual woman's attempt to formulate a self-defined femininity. Ultimately, duCille understands marriage as a "sign of the times that shifts with the times, the place, and the people, . . ." taking on "different social and political meanings for different historical subjects at different historical moments."[29]

Our examination of the romantic relationships at the center of the "Thug" series follows duCille's lead in reading marriage as a historically situated, politicized trope in African American women's writing. These relationships highlight two important characteristics of the politics of marriage in the era of transactional sexuality. The first is the persistence of the good woman/bad woman dichotomy, which is reframed in urban fiction through the opposing archetypes of the Bitch or the aspirational woman. The former is undesirable as a marriage partner while the latter is ideal. The second revelation is the way in which marriage and coupling continue to rely on and reproduce traditional gender relations and, thus, present obstacles to the attainment of female independence.

In the first novel, *Thugs and the Women Who Love Them*, the value of friendship and the importance of romantic relationships are articulated along with the notion of the independent woman. In the second book of the series, *Every Thug Needs a Lady*, the confluence of these relationships forms the substance of a congratulatory speech offered by Kyra as they start to realize some of the goals established in the first installment:

> My sisters, I think we all did pretty damn good. Even though we are all fine and beautiful we didn't get a man to depend on for food, clothing, and shelter. We handled our shit. . . . We put us first. . . . We can hold it down on our own if we have to. But for real, having a good man—another half—sure makes things a lot smoother. This toast goes to us. I love y'all, my sisters forever![30]

This passage's simultaneous emphasis on independence and desire for companionship is a crucial aspect of its difference from other black feminist discourses. It expresses hope that the answer to the question Morgan raises regarding whether the hip hop feminists' "equality" has rendered her "wholly undesireable" is a resounding NO! The valorization of marriage in these novels responds to fears which frequently are often unacknowledged in more conventional celebrations of female independence. They address the specter of abandonment and loneliness that many women fear may be a consequence of their "liberation." Even as urban fiction's reformulated marriage plot registers an attempt to evade "chronic singleness" it exposes the tendency of heterosexual coupling to reproduce the economic arrangements of transactional sexuality and reify traditional gender ideology that supports it. Ironically, the aspirational woman becomes the contemporary counterpart of traditional femininity, the nineteenth-century Angel of the House.

The idea that every thug needs a lady, captured in the title of the series' second installment, resonates with a nineteenth-century discourse of femininity as an ideological locus of moral purity. As celebrated in an early English description, the Angel of the House was a symbol of idealized femininity in which the female shone "like a beacon in a dark world" and was "a model of selflessness and purity of heart."[31] Responding to a rapidly changing economic order, its American iteration contrasted this notion of female selflessness and purity with the murky, public world of commerce inhabited by men. Both male protagonists of *Every Thug*, Trae and Kaylin, reflect a similar dynamic in their relationships with these "ladies." Notably, the beginnings of their romantic involvement with Roz/Tasha and Angel, respectively, coincide with their desire to get out of the sullied world of drug sales. However, their perception of their relationships contrasts that of the women. Where the women see their involvement with drug dealers as a contradiction of their career aspirations and social ambitions, the men value the women exactly because of their presumed distance from the world of drug dealing. As Trae and Kaylin discuss Kaylin's attraction to Angel, Kaylin declares: ". . . I may have just found my future wife. She's fine, smart, a square. She ain't a ho. A lawyer, not a chicken. Do you see where I'm going with this?"[32] Indeed, it is easy to follow Kaylin's logic as it is rooted in one of the oldest discourses of femininity in the world. Angel, as her name suggests, embodies the characteristics most desired in a wife under patriarchy.

Moreover, the novel also enacts a public/private split. Given the supposed centrality of their careers, the substance of the female characters' professional lives is given very little attention. Primarily, we witness the characters calling out sick from work or taking extended lunches so that they can meet their lovers for trysts. The minimal representation of the women's participation in the public world of work and their alignment with the moral legitimacy of the non-hustling world reproduces the broad strokes of the nineteenth-century discourse of the angel in the home and demonstrates that the social expectations regarding gender roles have not changed drastically in the twenty-first century. Instead, what is new is society's willingness to be explicit about the commodification of female sexuality, even as it calls it independence.

In spite of the hypocrisy of contemporary notions of female independence, it is important to acknowledge that the implications of transactional sexuality do not redound solely for conceptions of femininity. The value of traditional markers of ideal masculinity is also intensified under this regime. Hip hop culture embodies this intensification in the figure of the thug. A familiar explanation of the predominance of the thug persona in hip hop culture is that it is a figurative engagement of the black male quest for social power through its hyper-embodied emphasis on violent physical domination of other males and sexual conquest of females. This image is so pervasive that it has come to function for black and white audiences as a sign of authentic black identity. Typically, in this scenario the black male is understood to have been precluded from power on the basis of race. However, in *Black Sexual Politics*, Patricia Hill Collins offers an intersectional accounting of the dynamics of race, class, and generational affiliation which play out simultaneously in the thug persona.

Hill Collins argues that hip hop generation constructions of masculinity function politically as a rejection of the politics of assimilation ascribed to middle-class black masculinity. She problematizes the assumption of black male authenticity that underpin these dynamics, noting the historical origins of the association of black masculinity with hyper-embodiment, represented primarily in terms of superior sexual and athletic ability. Nonetheless, she makes a compelling case for understanding why thug masculinity resonates so strongly for working-class youth who have watched as middle-class black men "fail[ed] to defend African American interests because they fail to defy white male power. Instead, they tolerate and in many cases collude in reproducing the conditions in the inner city."[33] From the perspective of the hip hop generation, it may be difficult to see how legitimate power and racial solidarity can coexist.

In Clark's *Thug* novels the complex intersection of race and class in the thug persona is brought into focus by their exploration of the characteristics of male desirability, which, in turn, exposes the messy intersection of women's multiple desires. As these characters' aspirations for professional achievement and coupling conform to a fairly middle-class standard of success, their attraction to thugs must address some other aspect of their experience. In fact, it addresses one of the taboo subjects identified in Morgan's essay on hip hop feminism: the idea that women are attracted to the thug persona because those are the men who display power in a way that "makes our nipples hard."[34] In *Every Thug Needs a Lady* the narrative's central question is why thuggish masculinity is appealing to these women. At one point, Roz/Tasha literally asks her friends why they seem only to attract men who are "pimpin', slangin', bangin', and ballin'." In response, they point out that they are equally attracted to that kind of man, forcing her to admit her attraction to the aura of power exuded by thuggish men: "'That's what I like about Trae. He likes to run shit. Take over. I don't know about the next ho, but that shit turns me on,' laughed Roz. 'I know I don't want no weak-ass, pushover nigga.'"[35] Roz's initial framing of the question explicitly contrasted their preferred version of masculinity to professionals like "doctors; lawyers; (sic) investment bankers, and niggas like that . . ." intimating the hip hop generation's tendency to associate black male middle-class status with compromised black masculinity.

Though the characters express a preference for thug masculinity, it is not necessarily because they see such men as offering the kind of challenge to the status quo that Hill Collins has identified. Still, her analysis provides a useful framework for understanding the perception of desirable masculinity among hip hop generation men and *women*. Among this generation, masculine power and, thus, desirability is associated with exaggerated displays of wealth and physical dominance rather than other forms of social capital. The plot line involving Angel and her two suitors, drug-dealing Kaylin and Najee, a partner in the law firm at which she is interning, explicitly illustrates the competition of these two masculine ideals. Angel has expressed a desire to avoid becoming romantically involved with a drug dealer because of the risk of losing a mate to death, the penitentiary, or of compromising her own professional status through involvement with someone in a "complex occupation" and yet it is Kaylin, not Najee who captures her interest sexually. Choosing to act on this attraction, against her own best judgment, enmeshes Angel (and, similarly, her friend Roz/Tasha) in a web of contradictions.

In one passage, Roz/Tasha and Trae banter about which of them is the biggest player: "First of all I got my own money but I spend yours—rule #4. This is my house, but you and Nikayah been paying the note—#6. That 2000 Beamer parked out front, I got the title; it's in my name, but I didn't pay for it. And what year is this? 2000 nigga. Rule #9. I got a good job and cash stashed; I don't have to depend on y'all niggas for shit—rule #3."[36] Interestingly, Trae's version of the player rules focus on male monogamy: "'That's rule #9 in the playa's handbook: I'm not supposed to be sharin' this dick with nobody else . . .' 'Plus you ain't been burnin' or itchin': rule #7.'"[37] This banter casts Roz/Tasha in the traditionally masculine role of the pimp, who profits from the labor of others while Trae's articulation of monogamous sexuality is more closely aligned with the traditional expectations for female behavior. However, the reality is that a great deal of the narrative details how extravagantly these men woo the women—taking them on luxurious vacations, gifting them cash, cars and jewelry, and outfitting them in designer clothing in preparation for their dates. For instance, in preparation for one party, they begin at "a Gucci shop where Trae picked out a stomach-revealing black spider wrap for Tasha and a silk pin-striped miniskirt. She picked out a pair of black Jimmy Choo sandals and a bag to match. . . . Her tab came to $8,300."[38] The habit of detailing designer labels and the costs associated with them is consistent with hip hop expectation of a hyperbolic rendering of male power and attractiveness.

Ultimately, the strategy of achieving success through coupling is undermined by the inherent limitations of marriage and the women's own sexual desire. Coupling without a recalibration of both male and female gender ideologies is no more useful for formulating female independence than the deployment of bitchy black femininities. Such a recalibration would seek to create modes of masculine authority which did not depend on the symbols of power which, among the hip hop generation, are expressed in the thug persona.

BABY DADDIES AND THE DRAMA OF FAMILY PLANNING

Another arena in which urban fiction refracts the degree to which women's interests are subjected to an economy of male power is the issue of procreation. In the post–civil rights era of transactional sexuality, even parenting relationships have become politicized and monetized. Attributing problems such as the staggering rates of violence and unemployment among black youth to the demise of traditional family structures in black communities places the black family at the center of political debate. Meanwhile, the effort to hold men financially accountable as parents has led some states to dedicate special divisions of their social services departments solely to the enforcement of child support claims. Such responses reflect the reality that the number of black women-headed households, across the class spectrum, exceeds the number of households headed by white women by more than two to one.[39] The prevalence of this single-parent structure leads Morgan to observe that "Perhaps one of the most revolutionary acts the hip hop generation can accomplish is to establish healthy, loving, functional families."[40] In light of these "common sense" attitudes urban fiction's engagement of the struggle for control of female reproduction offers a salient point of entry for the black feminist scholar.

The call for such nuclear family units, while almost universally supported, is not without its complications. In *Gender, Race, and Nationalism in Contemporary Black Politics*, Nikol Alexander-Floyd argues that black political support for rhetoric of restored manhood and the nuclear family "enables both racist retrenchment in the country as a whole and sexist retrenchment in black communities."[41] Such rhetoric supports the racism which undergirds the black culture of pathology thesis and limits its potential to achieve the racial solidarity around which black politics are centered.[42] According to Alexander-Floyd these limits arise from the rejection of a black feminist frame of analysis—and its intersectional approach—in favor of bourgeois standards of success.[43] The kind of intersectional analysis championed by Alexander-Floyd would produce a class-based interrogation of black family formations that moved us beyond an uncritical valorization of the nuclear family. Further, it would account for the social and economic conditions that complicate the simple moralistic formulation on which the family restoration narrative depends, engendering an understanding of black familial structures that neither demonizes black women nor oversimplifies the role of fathers. Black male feminist, Mark Anthony Neal, points to the necessity of a critical examination of black fatherhood in *New Black Man*. Such an analysis, he argues, is a linchpin in the black male feminist project of "rethink[ing] their own masculinities and sexualities in order to create more productive relationships within the black community."[44]

Clark's *Thug* series, specifically, provides a useful starting place for identifying some of the questions that must be addressed in building the kind of feminist frame for understanding black family politics that Neal and Alexander-Floyd call for. Some questions which emerge out of an examination of these texts include: What does responsible fatherhood look like? What rights do men have to choose whether or not a pregnancy should be terminated? How might an assertion of such rights complicate the female quest for equity and independence? The answers to such questions complicate simplistic calls for the restoration of fatherhood or female independence and go a long way to explain why, in the era of transactional sexuality, the struggle for control over female reproduction has intensified.

In the *Thug* series this struggle is registered in the conflicts between men and women regarding when to conceive children or regarding women's decisions to terminate pregnancies. An example of the former is presented in *Thugs and the Women Who Love Them*. The character, Faheem, narrates his attempts to impregnate his girlfriend, Jaz, in spite of the fact that she has clearly expressed her desire to delay conception:

> She just want to finish school before she give me a baby. But I want a baby now. Because after she gets her Bachelor's degree, she going for her Master's. And knowing her, then she'll be on for her Ph.D. I say fuck that, we gotta have babies in between. She ain't gotta work nowhere and she can still keep going to school. That's why I don't be wearing no protection whenever I can get away with it. [45]

Faheem's near refusal to wear a condom demonstrates the degree to which women's ability to control the rate and timing of reproduction is subject to her male partner's authority. By the end of the first two novels in the series all four of the girlfriends have become pregnant or actually delivered a child, undermining their quest for independence by presenting obstacles to their professional advancement as well as their sexual pleasure. [46]

The female characters' unwillingness to be impregnated challenges the uncritical call for the restoration of the nuclear family structure. Yet, additional complications are brought to light in the aspects of the novels which represent the male perception that women have usurped their right to choose whether to terminate a pregnancy or not. Regarding men's rights as fathers, Morgan makes the provocative claim that "When it comes to admitting that . . . reproductive choice also grants women the power *to control the lives and destinies of unwilling fathers via their bodies,* feminism conveniently tosses the goal of a gender-equal society out the window." [47] The narrative registers the tension and mistrust that arise in such a political context through the representation of Roz/Tasha and Trae's conflicting perceptions of abortion. Because she has aborted one pregnancy for her previous boyfriend, Nikayah, Trae mistrusts Roz/Tasha. In contrast to Morgan's example, both

Trae and Nikayah seem to desire to become fathers. The sticking point is Roz/Tasha's failure to consult the potential father, reflecting the sense of inequality to which Morgan points. Trae's mistrust is further exacerbated by the fact that prior to his relationship with Roz/Tasha, another woman had attempted to entrap him by becoming pregnant. When he ends the, apparently casual, relationship, she terminates the pregnancy. Explaining to Tasha why she continues to call him, he tells her: "I used to fuck with her. She got pregnant, but at four and a half months, got an abortion. . . . Every so often she tries to get me to talk to her so that she can give me some bullshit story on why she killed my baby."[48] The anger and the sense of victimization apparent in his characterization of the events spill over into his relationship with Roz/Tasha, causing him to view her motives for choosing abortion with suspicion. While the reader may be able to sympathize with male vulnerability to women who either seek to entrap them or to deny their rights as fathers, these situations are no less indicative of female vulnerability.

As female independence depends in large part on economic self-sufficiency, ill-timed pregnancies represent a significant obstacle to its achievement. The reality of female economic vulnerability is, in fact, part of the logic of the family restoration narrative as it seeks, in part, to ameliorate the income inequalities that plague female-headed households. That logic is limited, however, to the extent that it frames paternity primarily in economic terms. As Neal points out, a truly progressive notion of fatherhood would be "about coming to terms with the lived experiences of black women and girls and imagining a world in which they can be the kinds of women—people—they want to be. . . ."[49] Given these parameters, we must read these characters' desire to be fathers against the grain, and suggest that they are less radical than they might initially appear.

Consider for example Trae's response to Roz/Tasha's concern that having a baby will delay her career plans: "I ain't goin' nowhere. We got money. We can work through this and get a live-in nanny so you still can do whatever you want to do. . . . Just trust me and have my baby, a'ight? Do you love me?"[50] Trae's sense that his only role as a father is to provide adequate financial resources, reduces even that relationship to a little more than a transaction. His response represents the difficulty many men face in imagining how they might contribute directly to the nurturance of a child. Thus, this exchange reinforces Neal's assertion that enabling black fathers to see themselves "as having something unique and important to offer" is a central project of black male feminism.[51]

On the whole, these novels guide the feminist critic toward a provocative problematization of fatherhood. Progressive black feminism is advanced by examining fatherhood in specific relation to the value for choice, to women's distinctive experiences as members of the black community and to ideal forms of parental engagement. Moreover, by addressing black women's experience from the perspective of the hip hop generation, urban fiction high-lights the need for theoretical perspectives which attend to popular culture, the tension between feminist theory and practice, and the unintended prolife-ration of paternalistic ideologies of masculinity. The themes addressed in this literature bridge the concerns of popular and academic feminism, pointing out the mutual concern with formulating functional models of female em-powerment that do not require women to deny their own fears or vulnerabil-ities. Finally, they prod us to recognize that black women's liberation is a communal project which requires the input of those within and without the ivory tower along with the support and activism of black men and women.

NOTES

1. Eve Dunbar, "Hip Hop (feat. Women Writers) Reimagining Black Women and Agency Through Hip Hop Fiction," in *Contemporary African American Literature: The Living Canon*, ed. Lovalerie King and Shirley Moddy-Turner (Bloomington and Indianapolis: Indian University Press), 108.

2. Tricia Rose, *The Hip Hop Wars: What We Talk About When We Talk About Hip Hop—and Why It Matters* (New York: Basic Books, 2008), 8.

3. Patricia Hill Collins, *From Black Power to Hip Hop: Racism, Nationalism, and Feminism* (Philadelphia: Temple University Press, 2006), 162.

4. Hill Collins, *Black Power*, 161.

5. Joan Morgan, *When Chickenheads Come Home to Roost: A Hip Hop Feminist Breaks is Down* (New York: Simon and Schuster, 1999), 57–58.

6. Morgan, *Chickenheads*, 56–57.

7. Here I am thinking of the multi-dimensionality associated with African Americans' use of the English language in ways that are succinct yet, simultaneously, communicative of a distinct perspective on the world and a philosophical measure of it. For a more detailed discussion, see Geneva Smitherman, *Talkin' and Testifyin': The Language of Black America* (Detroit: Wayne State University Press, 1985).

8. In *Black Noise: Rap Music and Black Culture in Contemporary America* (Hanover: University Press of New England, 1994), Tricia Rose argues that the impact of Robert Moses's Title I Slum Clearance program was a significant factor in the emergence of hip hop culture in the 1970s. Tactics of the war on drugs such as the development of gang member data bases, the implementation of three strikes conviction laws, and the militarization of public spaces in the 1980s and 1990s are understood by many to have contributed to the birth and popularity of West Coast gangsta rap. For detailed discussion see Pancho McFarland, *Chicano Rap: Gender and Violence in the Postindustrial Barrio* (Austin: University of Texas Press, 2008).

9. T. Denean Sharpley-Whiting, *Pimps Up, Ho's Down: Hip Hop's Hold on Young Black Women* (New York: New York University Press, 2007), 11.

10. Ibid., 118.

11. Ibid., 111.

12. Nick Chiles, "Their Eyes Were Reading Smut."

13. Hill Collins, 176.

14. Jacqueline Bobo, *Black Women as Cultural Readers* (New York: Columbia University Press, 1995), 5.

15. Tina McElroy Ansa, *You Know Better*, (New York: William Morrow, 2002), 114.

16. Vickie Stringer, *Let That Be the Reason*, (New York: Atria Books, 2009).

17. Cheryl Keyes, "Empowering Self, Making Choices, Creating Spaces: Black Female Identity via Rap Music Performance," in *That's The Joint: the Hip-Hop Studies Reader*, eds. Murray Forman and Mark Anthony Neal (New York: Routledge, 2004), 271.

18. Ibid., 272.

19. Sharpley-Whiting, *Pimps Up*, 144.

20. Ibid., 144.

21. Stringer, *Reason,* 16.

22. Elizabeth Marshall, Jeanine Staples, and Simone Gibson, "Ghetto Fabulous: Reading Black Adolescent Femininity in Contemporary Urban Street Fiction," in *Journal of Adolescent and Adult Literacy* 53/1(2009): 33.

23. Sharpley-Whiting, *Pimps Up*, 143.

24. Marshall, Staples, and Gibson, "Ghetto Fabulous," 34.

25. Stringer, *Reason*, 123.

26. Ibid., 123.

27. Wahida Clark, *Thugs and the Women Who Love Them* (New York: Kensington Publishing, 2005), 29.

28. Marshall, Staples, and Gibson, "Ghetto Fabulous," 33.

29. Ann duCille, *The Coupling Convention: Sex, Text, and Tradition in Black Women's Fiction* (New York: Oxford University Press, 1993), 4.

30. Wahida Clark, *Every Thug Needs a Lady* (New York: Dafina/Kensington, 2006), 3.

31. Sandra M. Gilbert and Susan Gubar, *The Madwoman in the Attic: The Woman Writer and the Nineteenth-Century Literary Imagination* (New Haven and London: Yale University Press, 1979), 22.

32. Clark, *Every Thug*, 113.

33. Patricia Hill Collins, *Black Sexual Politics: African Americans, Gender, and the New Racism,* (New York: Routledge, 2005), 176.

34. Morgan, *Chickenheads*, 58.

35. Clark, *Every Thug*, 9.

36. Ibid., 78–79.

37. Ibid., 78.

38. Ibid., 135.

39. Morgan, *Chickenheads*, 165.

40. Ibid., 166.

41. Nikol G. Alexander-Floyd, *Gender, Race, and Nationalism in Contemporary Black Politics* (New York: Palgrave Macmillan, 2007), 28.

42. This term refers to the idea that the social ills that plague many black communities are symptoms of those communities' inherent dysfunction. The perception of inverted power relations among men and women are supposed to reproduce a weak and ineffectual culture. Robin Kelley offers an exquisite critique of this sociological perspective in "Looking for 'the Real Nigga': Social Scientists Construct the Ghetto" in his *Yo' Mama's Disfunktional: Fighting the Culture Wars in Urban America,* (Boston: Beacon Press, 1997).

43. Alexander-Floyd, *Contemporary Black Politics*, 33.

44. Mark Anthony Neal, *New Black Man* (New York: Routledge, 2006), 64.

45. Clark, *Thugs and the Women Who Love Them*, 187.

46. Though female sexual pleasure does not fall directly into the purview of this essay, it is an important concern of in urban fiction and is commonly rendered in graphic detail.

47. Morgan, *Chickenheads*, 170.

48. Clark, *Every Thug*, 132.

49. Neal, *New Black*, 116.

50. Clark, *Every Thug*, 133.

51. Neal, *New Black*, 115.

Chapter Five

Hip Hop Tell-All Memoirs and Modes of Self-Construction

Recently, critics such as Eve Dunbar and T. Denean Sharpley-Whiting have offered some groundbreaking analysis of women's participation in hip hop culture. Bypassing the more traditional analytical perspectives on women as static objects constructed by the filmic gaze of hip hop music videos or the narratives of male potency presented in much of the lyrical content, these critics examine how women attempt to carve out spaces of agency through their production of fiction and through their actions as fans. I am deeply convinced of the importance of the arguments they offer and see them as stepping stones for my thinking about how black women engage some of the complexities of hip hop culture in their narratives. The exercises of power these critics reveal prompt my interpretation of hip hop memoir as socially consequential texts that contest the discourse on the black family in the neoliberal era.

In the previous chapter I discussed the ways in which I understand black women's production of urban fiction to create a dialogue with black feminist thought and the academy. In this chapter I will examine the ways in which the memoirs produced by hip hop generation black women engage yet another discursive sphere. In constructing their own personal narratives, these authors subvert the narratives of black family dysfunction that justified governmental withdrawal of social services in the late twentieth century. Their claims to titles such as Diva, Vixen, or even Hip Hop Helen of Troy, are complex reactions to deviant constructions of black female sexuality embodied in the iconography of the welfare queen, the video ho, or baby mama. By focusing on their attempts to manipulate their own self-images as well as the perceptions of others, their stories work to expose the oft-elided tensions between public and private relationships in the era of neoliberalism.

According to Mimi Abramovitz, "Neoliberal theory became dominant in the USA in the mid-1970s and extended the definition of the market from a simple system of exchange to include all processes of voluntary agreement among persons . . ."[1] Abramovitz goes on to describe that in actuality persons does not mean individuals but most frequently non-state entities such as the World Bank, the International Monetary Fund, and the World Trade Organization, whose voluntary agreements with developing or debtor nations frequently includes structural adjustment programs which presume that the "benefits of business-friendly neoliberalism will automatically trickle down to the average person."[2] This mode of philosophy which seeks to privatize many of the functions that had been, in the nineteenth and early twentieth centuries considered the responsibility of the state. These functions include the redistribution of wealth downward through taxation, providing income supplements to low-wage workers through social benefit programs, and the production of a properly socialized workforce through subsidies of women's unpaid labor in the home as the caretakers of children.

A move away from such a conceptualization of the state's responsibility necessarily has implications for individual citizens and the voluntary agreements undertaken by them. Those who study the cultural impact of neoliberal policy-making have identified the ways in which neoliberalism has produced significant contradictions for members of specific groups of individuals. Such contradictions become particularly pronounced in the arena of familial and sexual relationships since the latter are ostensibly private and the former are, presumably, voluntary and economically disinterested, in addition to being private. Each category is, of course, linked to the public life of the nation in various ways but neoliberalism is most frequently discussed in terms of "monetary and fiscal policy, trade negotiations, and economic indicators" thus obscuring the fact that it "in fact *has* a sexual politics . . ."[3]

In the analysis that follows, I want first to situate these memoirs as an important intervention in the public discourse on black female identity. Though they have most often been met with hostility from a various communities, reframing these texts as part of a particular black female discourse allows the reader to move beyond judgment of the character of the individual women and to see how they employ specific tropes and narrative strategies to reinsert the black female working-class voice into public conversations on family, sexuality, and the post-industrial economy. I take as examples Karinne Steffans *Confessions of a Video Vixen*, Carmen Bryan's *It's No Secret*, and Jacklyn "Diva" Bush's *The Gold Club*, a series of memoirs published between 2003 and 2007. I focus on these texts because they represent the earliest attempts by women to stake out a space from which to tell a collective story that challenges the public story of hip hop era black women. Though each author has been accused of presenting her story out of self-interest and an attempt "to make a quick buck," I do not think that their narratives should be so easily dismissed. Aside from the fact that most published authors hope to profit from their labor, I find such self-interest worthy of attention in a the context of systems of cultural production and social organization which are generally disinterested in or hostile to the black woman. Each text is steeped in the social context of early hip hop culture so that discourses of race, gender, and economics are never far from the discussion. Moreover, each of the texts engages notions of female agency—not necessarily through the actions recounted but through the act of recounting. These texts specify their audiences—either as young girls who must learn from the poor example set by Steffans, or the single mother's to whom Bryan dedicates her text of encouragement, or those who seek to understand the system of labor that structures the world of stripping which Bush's text exposes. Along with demonstrating how these narratives draw on and extend the tradition of black women's life-writing, I will examine how, thematically, they can be seen to constitute a dialogue with popular and political discourses on public policy and the social contract, specifically the intersection of work, morality, and sexuality which collide as a result of the consolidation of a neoliberal philosophy at the end of the century.

NEOLIBERAL RAINMAKING: BUSH AS DIVA

Most often the literature on hip hop culture emphasizes the deregulation of various media structures under the 1996 Telecommunications Act for the noticeable narrowing of the range of images of black men and women in hip hop culture down to what Tricia Rose calls the "Gangsta/Pimp/Ho nexus."[4] And surely such a view is legitimate. However, it may inadvertently erase the impact of other facets of neoliberal intervention which contribute to the emergence of such a strong discourse of gendered power exchanges; namely, the ways that other facets of media culture also contributes to the denigration of black female identity. For instance, we might understand the dominance of these tropes as not merely function of greedy corporate executives demands for more and more of these images to feed the consumer machine, but also as indications of how the artists in hip hop are responding to the larger social context (of which these deregulations are merely one facet) in which the social value of individuals as individuals is diminished and instead the value of individuals is increasingly defined in monetary terms.

Jacklyn Bush's memoir, *The Gold Club: the Jacklyn "Diva" Bush Story* is the first published of the three memoirs I examine in this chapter. Published in 2003, two years after the completion of the trial for fraud, prostitution, and charges of participation in organized crime, Bush's narrative is noteworthy because of what it represents as an early effort to shed light on the complicated ways in which the state, black sexuality, and neoliberal

contradictions between public and private intersect. The Gold Club as represented by Bush, offers an ideal model of the free market model espoused by
neoliberal philosophy, and her attention to the operation of the club nearly
overshadows the personal narrative. In fact, the first third of the narrative is
devoted to detailing the business model of Gold Club and the income opportunities it provided for it various categories of employees. Within the first
one hundred pages, Bush has described the corporate model which structured
the operation of the Gold Club; detailing, for instance, how the dancers were
taught to interact with customers through role-playing exercises which took
place at Sunday afternoon company meetings, the pink-slip system of accounting for champagne sales (by which the "entertainers" earned bonuses)
or the costing scheme for activities in the private rooms. Providing such
detail helps to emphasize the idea that the Gold Club was, in fact, a retail
enterprise with practices drawn from more mundane customer service oriented environments such as corporate restaurants, which rely too on up-selling,
promotional activities, and "personalization" strategies. The distinction between her place of employment and others is not moral distinction but rather
the distinctive earning opportunities presented by the Gold Club. She recounts how she was sometimes able to make as much as $10,000 in a single
night and her efforts to teach her fellow entertainers to acquire the skills that
they needed to be able to also earn well.[5]

In combination, Bush's celebration of owner Steve Kaplan's business
practices and the picture of the earning potential she describes might seem
like an advertisement for the neoliberal theory of "trickle-down" economics.
According to trickle-down's proponents, policies that favor corporations and
the wealthy also provide opportunities for the less well-off because of the
spending they generate. Similarly, the spending of the mostly wealthy clientele of professional athletes, actors, and media moguls enabled women and
men like Jacklyn Bush, with little prospect for high earnings to enjoy the
vaunted middle-class American dreams of suburban home-ownership, family
vacations, and good education for their children.[6]

As noted earlier, the neoliberal paradigm carries in it many inherent
contradictions. Primary among them is the effacement of race, class, and
gender as simultaneous aspects of both private (individual) and public (social) identity. Bush's narrative reflects this tension. On the one hand, she
strives to present her work at the Gold Club as primarily an instrument of
personal autonomy allowing her to become "Diva." In the early sections of
the book her identity as Diva overshadows the story of her childhood as if
she is unwilling to acknowledge that, to some extent, her labor in the Gold
Club is linked to her origins "in the heart of the ghetto" as the daughter of a
waitress turned drug-addict mother and a line-cook turned serial philanderer
who only came home to beat her mother.[7] When she does acknowledge the
impact of her childhood on her development as she does when she states: "As

a little girl, watching my mother, I was learning a lot, fast. . . . Basically, in my mind, it seemed that it was a man's world and my place, as a female, was second" she does not really offer an examination or explanation of how such early lessons might be related to her professional life.[8] In fact the structure she chooses to tell her story—alternating one or two chapters of the Gold Club material with a single chapter in which she recounts painful childhood or early adult memories—creates one continuous, basically, chronological narrative of her Gold Club life that is juxtaposed with what, sometimes, reads as a random assortment of traumatic episodes from her early years. I read this structure as indicative of her real life attempt to superimpose a coherent powerful female identity over the gender binary she has witnessed as a child.

Her identity as Diva is the subject of much reflection in the memoir and reflects Aisha Lockridge's take on the diva figure in African American literature as one who "is not about loss; she is about finding herself and loving her."[9] Bush's examination includes some description of how she acquires the name, what it means to her and even some critique of her own Diva behaviors. One way in which Bush rejects the loss paradigm is in her relationship to her stage name and her real name. She explains that before working at the Gold Club, she used her own name, Jackie: "I believed if you were a dancer you should be proud of what you do and not be embarrassed by covering up your name."[10] In this way, Bush refuses to submit to the "ho stigma" that so often undermines the power that many women seek through the labor as strippers. However, in Atlanta, she accepts the name Diva, which was chosen for her by others who "said it was very independent and strong and it suited [her] because they looked to [her] as a leader."[11] Rather than a loss of identity, it seems to represent a synthesis of her personal and professional identities. Still, she does not give up her identity as Jackie and in fact suggests that her willingness to tell her customers her real name was central to building her clientele since it helped her to build relationships with them—a significant aspect of her professional status as Diva.

She is much less equivocal about accepting the connotation of leadership and independence associated with the name Diva. Though she names many of the celebrities who came into the club, Bush seems not to have been starstruck for very long. Her main interest is in making money and that is related to two of her main skills, as she reports it. Those skills were selling champagne and knowing "what was wanted [by individual customers] and who [among the entertainers] would give it."[12] Together, these skills allowed her to increase her earning from tips for helping match the client with the right dancer, avoid dancing herself unless she wanted to, and enjoy a status of unquestionable authority within the club, all of which help her to counterbalance her childhood sense that there were no opportunities for women to exercise control in a man's world.

Bush's "Diva" tale exposes the interstices of the public private split that is assumed by neoliberalism. Her story is in many ways indicative of an entire social experience. In her exploration of her identity as Diva, she shows how what is presumably a commercial persona develops in relationship to the basic facts of her private identity as a poor black woman in the racial-sexual landscape of post-industrial America. That landscape is one in which race signifies in slippery ways. While certain patterns of racial inequality structure Bush's childhood world, the status and centrality of black men to the Gold Club clientele seems proof of some kind of post-racial dream. That dream is, of course, intimately linked to neoliberal philosophy which is frequently justified by the notion that the problems of economic disparity along the axis of race or gender have been addressed by civil rights legislation and affirmative action and thus no longer require the intervention of the state to ensure adequate economic protections and opportunities for groups with less power historically.

The proximity of these black women writers to men who exercise a relatively high degree of power in the contemporary social landscape works to submerge any very strong racial analysis but heightens their attention to questions of gender and sexuality since the "characters" are relating from those specific contexts. This attention to a specifically gendered experience is one that links all three of the texts I'm examining here. Ironically, race is a category which each deals with by sleight of hand. Instead of addressing the impact of race directly, these narratives engage specific tropes that reflect the complexity of racial discourse in the twenty-first century. Bush's narrative challenges the public policy construction of black women as powerless, dependent drains on the state by projecting her Diva identity, focusing on the economics of sex (work), and downplaying her own blackness while emphasizing her mother's whiteness.

She makes several interesting observations regarding her mother that contribute to my reading of her text as a challenge to the public narrative about black women, work, and welfare. Bush highlights her mother's white face as her own personal icon of dependence, noting that "We were on welfare and never got off of it my whole childhood"[13] and that her mother was often the only white woman in any neighborhood in which they lived. Aside from challenging the association of welfare dependency with black women, Bush's construction of her mother's and her own hopeless marriages lead her away from the government's spin on marriage as a salve for economic woes of the late twentieth century. Stripping, not marriage, is the route that Bush perceives as leading to financial and emotional autonomy. Her father made little financial contribution to the family and whatever contribution he did make came at the cost of various abuses including beatings "with his fists, a baseball bat, whatever was close at hand" or his supplying her dependence on a variety of drugs. Similarly, when Bush is forced by her father to marry (because she had become pregnant) her husband quickly begins to repeat the pattern of infidelity and financial dependence that she had witnessed as a child.

It is in this context then, that Bush's focus on the Gold Club as a plum labor option becomes so significant. Given that Bush would not have been able to count on the kind of support that was available to women in her mother's era, that the kinds of labor options that were available to her when she entered into the workforce at seventeen were low-paying jobs in a pizza shop or as a home health aid, the opportunity represented in the strip clubs becomes a much more attractive alternative to the supposedly more moral pursuit of marriage that the state was promoting as the main social safety net for young women at the time of Bush's coming of age.

When compared to either marriage or the forms of employment that were otherwise available to her Bush chooses stripping as the most personally empowering form of employment. And it is her exploration of her economic experience that makes her text a significant contribution to the record of black women's experience in the context of post-industrial neoliberalism. It exposes the hierarchies of race and gender that are elided by the assumption of a market that operates independently of other social structures as well as the logical impossibility of truly distinct public and private spheres. Her examination of the blurred boundaries between the personal and professional lives of strippers demonstrates the ways in which public, market-based notions of power frequently intersect "private" arrangements.

Exposing the blurred lines between the public world of work and the private, domestic, world, Bush's narrative illustrates the nexus of contradictions and overlap among "regular relationships" and their dynamics of power and exchange and those of the strip club. She notes that one of the dangers of stripping is that one begins to feel that "everybody [in your life outside of the strip club] owes you something even if you're just sitting there talking with somebody."[14] Even personal relationships with a boyfriend or husband can be colored by the idea that, because the stripper is sleeping with him, "he needs to be taking care of [her]."[15] Bush frames this as a bleeding over of the money for time dynamic of the strip club into the personal realm. Even when one does not have the expectation that the male partner be the one who's paying for things, this dynamic of exchange can creep into the relationship. She relates another distortion that can occur as a result of the dynamics of exchange in the stripping world in which giving money in personal relationships can become an assertion of independence for the female partner. She explains that instead of trying to find a sugar daddy many strippers want "somebody underneath her that she can take care of. If she had a man with oodles of money, she wouldn't have her independence."[16] Bush, herself, critiques both the expectation of being taken care of or the desire to be the one taking care as antithetical to an egalitarian partnership. Interestingly, though, she attributes the problem to "getting caught up" so that "you can't distinguish between being a dancer and dealing with outside life."[17] While Bush attributes the inequities of her relationship to contamination by the values of the stripping lifestyle, she does not make the connection that the strip club merely exaggerates the gender norms of mainstream society. The club may put these dynamics into stark relief but if women's bodies and sexuality were not already socially constructed as totems of male social power, it would be nearly impossible to establish multi-million dollar businesses predicated on such a premise.

The majority of the text demonstrates that in some fundamental ways the Gold Club, at least, was not qualitatively different from other business enterprises. Though, of course, many would look askance at the highly sexualized environment of the Gold Club, the state of Georgia did not. In fact, some of the details that Bush provides help to illuminate that the state saw stripping mainly as an economic enterprise rather than an assault on the social good or morals of its citizens. For instance she notes that Georgia is the only state that permits the sale of alcohol alongside complete nudity, she describes the rather lenient licensing process for adult entertainment workers (an industry that she claims, in Atlanta, was second only to Coca Cola's enterprises), and she notes that the adult entertainment industry is intimately linked to the city of Atlanta's popularity as a convention locale. I make note of these details to suggest that a willingness to commodify women's sexuality is, in fact, a mainstream value, not the sole purview of the strip club. It is important to pay attention to this contradiction because acknowledging that such gender and power dynamics permeate all spheres of our culture makes it more difficult to bracket off such exchanges as the particular purview of black women who have been historically constructed as morally loose and willing participants in the commodification of their own sexuality and held solely responsible for systems of exchange that are structured by and depend upon extended networks of social support.

Moreover, the circumstances of the publication of Bush's memoir demonstrate the impact of a racial hierarchy which also belies the notion of a market free of social hierarchies. Bush's memoir is published by Milligan Books an apparently small press operating out of a strip mall in south Los Angeles. Milligan Books is listed in an online business directory, but has no independent web presence, no list of its catalog, and little to indicate that it is more than a "vanity" press. Given the national coverage garnered by the Gold Club trial, it is surprising that no mainstream press would be interested in Bush's story which includes references to celebrity clients ranging from Keanu Reeves to Ted Turner, Dennis Rodman, Madonna, and even Robin Leach. One can only conclude that presses such as Miramax or Seal Press, with its particular address of female consumers, could not imagine the same widespread audience interest in such a narrative by a black women as they did when publishing narratives with similar themes by white women authors. As T. Denean Sharpley-Whiting suggests, it demonstrates "black women's marginality in our understanding of the strip trade" as Bush's is the only non-white voice amongst a slew of stripper's memoirs which were published between 2001 and 2005.[18] This lack of interest in the black women's take on the strip club has much to do with the general perception of black women's sexuality as deviant. While white women's tales can be pitched either as manifestos of feminist liberation or apologias for "good girls gone wrong," black women's experiences are rendered "pedestrian, mundane, and unmarketable" by the generally held assumptions of hypersexuality and questionable morality.[19]

Ultimately, Bush's story illuminates the opportunities and limitations of stripping as one of the routes to independence available to working-class women of the post-industrial era. Her narrative exposes the degree to which the earnings potential of the strip club, while a compelling contrast to lower paying service work, does not ultimately challenge either the hierarchies of gender that frame sexual relations between men and women or the larger economic dynamics that create the rigidly defined patterns of labor and earnings that limit the economic potential of many women in the first place. However, her attention to her work as *work* minimizes the potential for negative moral judgments of Bush, since she is a good employee, working for a company that embodies the most widely accepted capitalist principles of the day—the market as its own moral standard.

BLACK WOMEN AND THE VOICE OF JUDGMENT

As I have suggested earlier in this chapter, the rise of neoliberal economic policy assumed a certain leveling of "the playing field" in the post–civil rights era, presumably removing the need for state protections of historically disempowered groups. I'd like, now, to describe how such assumptions amounted, in particular policy situations, to de facto attacks on black women. In the case of welfare policy reform, for instance, the shift in attitude regarding that state's obligations,[20] had a particular impact on African American women's economic prospects, some of which I've discussed above in relation to Bush's economic prospects. Here, though, I'd like to draw attention to the discursive attack on black women that was used to legitimize such reforms as the Personal Responsibility and Work Opportunity Reconciliation Act (PRWORA). Political science scholar, Nikol Alexander-Floyd argues that the Personal Responsibility and Work Opportunity Reconcilation Act of 1996 "was passed because of the power of the mythology around Black Welfare Queens and the breakdown of the Black family."[21] Moreover, this mythology reflected a politics of disgust and constructed black women as sexually loose and morally undisciplined. The reforms were presented as antidote to the natural tendencies of the "black culture of poverty" and offered black women an opportunity to discursively align with the "positive values" of self-sacrifice, social conformity, and the discipline of abstinence.[22]

It is in the context of such dehumanizing discursive attacks on black women generally that I read Steffans's 2005 memoir *Confessions of a Video Vixen* in which she details her liaisons with various rap industry figures through her work first as a stripper and video model, and then as professional "groupie." Though there have been debates about the accuracy of Steffans's tales and some questions about whether she is a victim or an exploiter, I am interested less in the memoir as a representation of one individual's true experience and more interested in how the narrative (as truth or fiction) is in dialogue with the discursive construction of black women in the moment about which she's writing.

I see this dialogue as an important part of a distinctly feminine black counter-public sphere. In this perception, I am drawing on a variety of scholarly analyses that describe black women's writing as political activism (Patricia Hill Collins, for instance) as well as the work of M. Harris-Perry and Nicole Floyd Alexander, both of whom describe the ways in which the patriarchal nature of black liberation movements has excluded women's voices and perspectives from the black public sphere. Consequently, I am interested in how Steffans frames her narrative in a way that claims space for a black woman's voice in a historical moment in which the working class black woman's image was a construction of almost anyone but herself. I want to emphasize that I'm not arguing that Steffans's narrative responds directly to welfare policy, but rather that it is in dialogue with a particular public discourse about black femininity that was tied to the politics of welfare reform. However, since the avenues of self-representation were particularly limited for working-class black women, Steffans's assertive self-representation becomes particularly meaningful in its claims to personal and individual subjectivity in the context of social objectification of black femininity.

Steffans's narrative strategy is notable for the way it attempts to manage multiple ethical perspectives. Instead of trying to make economic sense of the choices she made, Steffans offers a portrait of herself as an individual isolated from any sustaining sense of self or community and, thus, enacts a narrative that is almost the opposite of Bush's. Steffans's attempts to trade in sexual fantasy work directly against her struggle for personal autonomy specifically because they are entirely private and therefore not recognized as a form of labor. The difference in her narrative strategy and Bush's is interestingly captured in her choice of the term vixen, which gets at some of the distinctions between Steffans' quest for power and Bush's. The term vixen carries the connotation of craft or manipulation traditionally associated with foxes. Similarly, the human female who is typically described as a vixen is seen as gaining any advantages she may have through wile, manipulation, or trickery. Unlike the Diva, the vixen's claims to power are seen as predatory rather than authoritative and legitimate. The diva deserves her power because she exercises the creativity, self-regard, and strength to flaunt a system that would disempower her. On the other hand, the vixen exercises power that she has wrested from others through her craftiness so she is perceived differently from the diva. The titles these women adopt to name their identities reflect a fundamental difference in their self-perception. Naming herself as vixen is consistent with Steffans's repudiation of her past life. That position of dis-avowal is a necessary strategy for gaining the sympathy of her audience and holding it long enough for them to listen. The need to create sympathy in the audience is coextensive with her ongoing attempt to forge a sustaining iden-tity which the role of vixen could not provide. In narrating her life, she is literally attempting to remake herself. In taking such an approach, Steffans works in tandem with a longer tradition of black women's life writing to the extent that she chooses to subordinate direct engagement of social issues and structures to an examination of personal trauma that stem from such social mechanisms. In this way she participates in a black rhetorical tradition of challenging the social system obliquely by asserting one's humanity in a context of dehumanization. This strategy has been particularly associated with women's writing. [23]

Though Steffans's memoir is primarily concerned with her individual remaking, it, nonetheless, exhibits a social dimension. The stated goal of her text is to warn other young girls away from the lifestyle that she had chosen by elucidating the many pitfalls that can occur when the vixen loses control of the game she is playing. While such a goal is, perhaps, belied by Steffans's follow up publication *The Vixen's Manual: How to Find, Seduce and Keep the Man You Want*, I would argue that Steffans's first publication is worthy of consideration because of its willingness to engage what are widespread social traumas. Her narrative engages the unique psychic, material (and, sometimes, physical) violence to which women of her generation have been subjected. While African American women have always been subjected to a variety of demeaning discourses about their identities, no other generation has had to negotiate them in a context filled with so many contradictions. Historically, supposed black sexuality (both male and female) has not been simultaneously a source of social denigration and a globally celebrated source of economic mobility, a symbol of personal autonomy and the subject of social policy, a marker of cool and a source of mainstream cultural prac-tices. In this context, her frank discussions of her failed relationships and her social alienation demonstrate the difficulty of contemporary negotiations of black identity.

Her connection to the hip hop industry is central to decoding the contradictory gender politics of post–civil rights African American identity. While the industry provides opportunities for black male economic and discursive power, the opportunities it provides for women are rather more limited. For women, the main point of entry into the rap music industry—the most prominent and lucrative aspect of hip hop culture—is through some form of sexual performance. By trading on their images as sexual objects many women find opportunities to work in the hip hop sphere. However, while some find the economic and social opportunities they are seeking, many others run headlong into the limitations of its reactionary gender politics. This trajectory is traced out in Steffans's account of the project of self-invention that she undertook first in the strip club through her alter ego Yizette Santiago and then when she attempted to remake herself as the sexual fantasy, Superhead. Being based either on the premise of self-evasion (a form of deception) or self-objectification (manipulation), both fail.

Her relationship with Kool G Rap provides a case in point regarding her failure to successfully realize her effort to carve out an autonomous space. She met him while working as a stripper—a role in which she had become pretty successful, mastering distinctive and acrobatic moves and making up to $1,000 a shift. Since she was working as a stripper, she gave him the name under which she danced; her alter ego Yizette Santiago. Entering into the relationship under this identity, deeply imbricated in hierarchical gender relations, seems to guarantee that none of her expectations for her self-development can be met. Instead, she depicts it as a relationship defined by his authority as a male. Once he declares her his "wife" the trajectory for her is a loss of power that is symbolized by his desire for her to call him Daddy. She says, "it was difficult to for [her] to let anyone tell [her] what to do and even more difficult for [her] to give someone a title of authority."[24] She does resist at first, but eventually comes to submit.

In submitting to his desire Steffans's loses the authority to define herself—one which she had been attempting to exercise through her alter ego Yizette Santiago, the name she used as a stripper. Interestingly, it is her age and the fact that all of her documents carry this name that prevents her from being legally married to him, as she explains it. I find this issue of naming intriguing because this alter ego is simultaneously connected to her self-assertion since it is stripping that allows her break with her father and still support herself and which prevents her from becoming Kool G's wife, legally. On the other hand, it also captures the loss of self that Jacklyn Bush rejected, because it masks rather than enables her identity as Karinne Steffans.

After she finally breaks with the abusive Kool G, Steffans's does not give up the strategy of trying to trade her sexuality for security. In fact, as she transitions into video "modeling" she tries on yet another new identity and earns the name Superhead. This moniker refers to her skill at fellating men but it also resonates with the idea of Chickenhead. The latter, of course, also has an association with the act of fellatio, but it is a derogatory term. Steffans's nickname was supposed to be a symbol of power. It was bestowed upon her by Ja Rule, after a sexual encounter which she describes thus: "I had him there in my mouth, and in those moments I was a beast . . . I had him, I knew it. What I was doing to his body was new to him and especially to me . . . I was powerful at this moment. I'd discovered something new—I had the power here."[25] Steffans has misread her power and her control over her identity. The nickname, Superhead, which arose from a joking reference to a line in a Jadakiss song, "quickly turned into [her] scarlet letter" and, in her estimation, "would be taken out of context from that day forward."[26] As the narrative progresses she continues to be involved with Ja Rule and a number of different figures in the music world including Fred Durst of Limp Bizkit and "Papa" the pseudonym she assigns to a married man whose identity she wants to protect. None of them makes the kind of permanent commitment she is seeking and her reputation worsens. Though she depends on their financial contributions to her life, these relationships are also about her "overwhelming need to prove [her] worthiness."[27]

Her biography offers many reasons that she might feel less than worthy. Her childhood was riddled with conflict with her mother, who resented her as a symbol of her own failed relationships. She was brutally raped at an early age and her father's involvement in her life was of a "last resort" variety. When coupled with such experiences, the general discourse on black women emanating from the media could work to validate her feelings of unworthiness. That is, her individual trauma would be normalized by the representations of black women that suggested they were loose and radically in need of discipline. In this light, her attempt to cultivate sympathy for her experiences deserves recognition.

This aspect of Steffans's narrative—her willingness to tell a story that an audience will likely greet with skepticism—links her to a tradition of black women's writing. One particularly provocative example of this connection with other black women's writing is presented in novelist Tayari Jones's 2005 blog post on *Confessions*. Jones, compares the memoir to Harriet Jacobs's *Incidents in the Life of a Slave Girl*, suggesting that both subject—Steffans and Jacobs—have to negotiate a powerful set of cultural assumptions about their sexuality as black women and are thus linked by the courage it takes to tell the stories of their lives in the context of a culture which routinely "traffics in women's bodies." In addition to exhibiting courage similar to Jacobs's, Steffans also utilizes some of the same sentimental narrative strategies to cultivate reader sympathy.

The lessons that Steffans learns from these exchanges of identities and power are presented as a cautionary tale for other young girls thinking of such negotiations. Consistent with the sentimental tradition, the lessons of the text are to be learned from the emotional experience rather than any direct argument against Steffans's choices. Consequently, Steffans's tale relies heavily on pathos. One of the most poignant instances comes at the beginning of the text, when she narrates the experience of hitting bottom. She is in the one-stall bathroom of a chic Hollywood restaurant overdosing.

> The last thing I remembered was my body shaking violently as I sat on the toilet with my head in my hands and my friend Eva hovering over me asking if I was okay. . . . The next thing I knew, I was on the floor again. When I came to from another bout of convulsions, my tongue was swollen and bloody . . . I desperately wanted someone to walk in and help, but no one came. [28]

In this passage, Steffans's isolation is total. The space contains her physically, she can't control her body, and her memory is failing her so that there is no aspect of herself to which she can lay claim. This rendering of her as an isolated body is one that is repeated throughout the text, and I read it as highly resonant with the kind of social alienation of black women as a whole that is embedded in the pro-reform discourse of the era. The shift from welfare as social benefit and obligation to the perception of it as a drain on society was tied to a discursive construction of welfare recipients as primarily black (in spite of the fact that as a percentage, the number of black people as recipients diminished between 1969 and 1994) achieved a kind of symbolic isolation of the black female. Moreover, this racialization of welfare discourse allowed decision makers to construct an us vs. them discourse which positioned welfare "recipients as a threat to society with their false claims of entitlement"[29] and made their efforts to survive a target of social censure.

Ultimately, Steffans's memoir represents an important instance of speaking from the position of one who is economically, socially, and morally, disenfranchised. As a member of the hip hop generation, she is dually positioned in relation to a historical figure like Jacobs as well as to the presumptive "welfare queen" targeted by the discourse of "personal responsibility" in her own era. Julia Jordan-Zachery defined the welfare queen as a rhetorical construction of working-class black femininity which represents them "in a particular way that relies on historical referential strategies, discursive practices and statements" the result of which was that they "often do not receive the opportunity to speak for themselves." Since we rarely hear black women telling their own stories—either in political culture or popular cultural forms like hip hop—by telling her story Steffans is finally exhibiting the sense of worth that she had been seeking the relationships she details. Thus, as Steffans herself says, telling her story is not shocking because she's has sex with many different men, "the shocking part is that [she's] talking about it."[30]

MORE THAN HIS BABY MAMA

In the wake of the ideological shift away from social collectivism that characterizes much of the 1980s and 1990s, many poor young people of color found themselves pushed to participate in illicit economies and/or extend the tradition of informal entrepreneurialism in working-class black communities. For many males, this meant hustling drugs or hustling narratives of the drug life through rap music. Women, finding themselves largely excluded from both of these arenas, nonetheless, find ways to avail themselves of the income that is being generated out of these alternative economies. Since the public world of work available in the post-industrial economic context was one that excluded women in various ways, young black women found themselves in the fairly unprecedented position in which coupling became the most likely source of economic stability. One significant way in which they were able to do so was through the formation of sexual/romantic/familial relationships with the most successful males they could. Hip hop culture developed its own parlance for describing such relationships—"wifing" a woman is to assign a position of primacy; chickenheads are women with whom to engage in more casual and transitory sexual relations in which fellatio is the most frequent form of sexual activity. In each case the language reflects the agency of the male and obscures the fact that the female position has an accompanying scale of compensation. The contributions that men are expected to make, provide exactly the kinds of subsidies that the state used to be responsible for; making it possible for women to obtain some of the necessities or even the "extras" that they might otherwise lack access to. Though "wifey" is a more elevated position than that of a chickenhead it, too, can be quite transitory and women involved in such relationships often see producing children as a strategy to help secure a more permanent position. Thus, the phenomena of the Baby Daddy/Baby Mama.

The sociological phenomena which are captured in this various nomenclature have entered into the broad cultural lexicon to the extent that they function archetypally. In the context of rap music narrative, we have been exposed to these ideas primarily from a male perspective, as captured in songs such as Kanye West's "Goldigger," or Outkast's "Ms. Jackson," which both comment on these dynamics. These archetypes and characterizations loom large in the written form associated with hip hop—urban fiction and tell-all memoirs. However, they are distinctive in that they tend to come from a female point of view and to offer a take on these coupling relations which emphasizes the larger social conditions that frame working class black women's attempts to achieve economic stability and personal autonomy via strategic partnering.

Carmen Bryan's *It's No Secret* is, ostensibly, a memoir aimed at setting the record straight regarding her overlapping relationships with Nas and

Jay-Z, which erupted in a public feud between the two rappers in 2000—making her the hip hop Helen of Troy. This incident was driven by Jay-Z's leaking of hints about their relationship in his verse on Memphis Bleek's, "Is That Your Chick?" However, Bryan's narrative shifts perspective from her sexuality as an object of competition between the two rappers and centralizes her own quest for self-fulfillment. Her account of these relationships is framed in terms of how the men either inhibit or advance that quest. The narrative gives particular attention to the negotiation of and unsuccessful attempt to transform her relationship with her Baby Daddy, Nas, from an informally recognized alliance to a contractually defined and legally sanctioned marriage.

In her recounting of their relationship she takes control of the narrative by contrasting the distinctions between marrying and "wifing." In the former, as Bryan conceives it, there is parity among the partners while the latter offers a much more patriarchal understanding of the familial relationship. Although feminism has explored the ways in which formally recognized marriage relationships may be structured by gender imbalance, Bryan's narrative exposes the even greater disparities that attend less formal family relationships. As she understands it, the absence of a legal contract enables Nas, the father of her child, to maintain sexual and economic autonomy in their relationship, even as they remain bound by their shared parenthood. In order to assure his commitment to their family, she is compelled for much of their relationship to maintain sexual and emotional fidelity to him, while he is able to exercise sexual freedom and emotional availability at levels of his own choosing. When Bryan finally begins to assert her own interests by pursuing other more emotionally satisfying relationships, he withdraws financial support of their child. Thus, Bryan's narrative exposes the greater social vulnerability that accrues to the Baby Mama, who lacks the kind of social structure of expectation that would support the claims of a legally recognized partner. Though Bryan's narrative ends with her having secured a legal order of financial support for her child, other aspects of her life experience emphasize the significance of the particular historical moment of social and economic shift in shaping her experience as a black women at the turn of the twenty-first century. Her story registers the limited horizon of expectation for black youth in the post–civil right/post-industrial era and the importance of state provisions for the security of its citizens.

Bryan's text can be read as an attempt to reclaim the notion of family from the informal system of family that developed in the post-industrial era. To that end, she constructs her mother as an icon of a bygone era to whom her own romantic relationships stand in stark contrast. Her mother, for instance, grew up in a neighborhood "with a diverse makeup of blue collar workers, musicians, doctors, and lawyers."[31] She attributes to her mother a kind of naked ambition and work ethic that makes sense for someone of the civil rights era but seems less tenable for working-class youth of the post-soul/post-industrial era in which the fruits of such labor are not as evident and she concludes that "Overworking and overextending yourself were for my mother's generation."[32] By the time that Carmen Bryan comes of age, for instance, the socially legitimized well-paying employment options she can see are associated with the entertainment industry and the kinds of mixed-income neighborhoods in which her mother came of age are few and far between. Instead what she sees is the social landscape of the ghetto structured by the crack economy. She notes "By the end of high school, just about everyone I knew either sold crack, had a boyfriend who sold crack or actually was on crack."[33] Thus it appeared to her, as to many others, that hustling "was a regular job with bigger payoffs than bagging groceries down at Fine Fare" and she decides to link her fate with that of a hustler.[34]

Almost immediately, though, she begins to learn of the instabilities associated with the role of a hustler's girl. First, her drug-dealing boyfriend is incarcerated and then while visiting him in jail she discovers that he has an ongoing relationship with "the family he'd assured [her] was out of the picture." She comes to the realization that she could never expect a hustler to settle down with just her as multiple women seem to be a part of the hustler lifestyle. Soon after these incidents she begins dating Nas. At that time Nas's career was still on the ascent and the trajectory of their relationship reveals the continuities and contradictions of family relationship cemented by biology rather than law. He proposes to her immediately but never marries her, she becomes impregnated by him, but they terminate two pregnancies before she gives birth to their daughter, Destiny.

Rather than embrace the role of Baby Mama, Bryan's narrative emphasizes her competence and commitment to a more formalized notion of family, over any sense of easy dependence on Nas. Throughout she seems to purposefully construct her own role as one that should have merited more than the minimal financial commitment of Baby Daddying. Their relationship as she represents it reveals the limitations of the microstructure of the family as it relies on distorted "definitions and operations of manhood and womanhood."[35] In presenting her potential as a marriage partner, Bryan rejects the narrative of female dependence. Her competence is highlighted in the attention that she pays to her laboring in public, first for Russell Simmons's Def Jam Records and then for Tracey Waples, then a senior vice president of A & R at Capitol Records. She emphasized not only her value to the function of these places of employment, but also that often it was her pay that supported their family. Their contrasting sensibilities expose Nas's conservative gender politics in relation to his parenting, his views of what is appropriate behavior for her, and in terms of the organization of the social lives.

One of the shorthands she creates for describing Nas's style of parenting is the title of "Uncle Daddy" which she and her female relatives had bestowed upon him. Nas, as conveyed through her memory has little capacity to father beyond his economic contributions. Even when he is at home, he offers her very little support in the role of parenting. In one passage she recounts his refusal to even be responsible for their child even briefly while she filled a prescription for medicine for their sick child. In contrast to many other memoirs of the genre Bryan's record takes a distinctly anti-materialistic cast. She frequently points out how little Nas's attempts to purchase, rather than earn his role in the family, mean compared to the gift of time that she repeatedly requests. After she attempts to take her own life, he presents her with a platinum tennis bracelet, and this marks the turning point that will lead up to her relationship with Jay-Z. She despaired of ever making him understand that what she "really desired was his time" and commits herself to meeting her own needs.

However, her attempt to meet her own needs is constrained by his sense of what constitutes proper female behavior and his constant policing of her actions. His attitude is informed by his somewhat antiquated notion of female gender roles. As Bryan describes it "His idea of the ideal woman was pregnant, barefoot, and in the kitchen."[36] These archaic attitudes are also reflected in their gender segregated social lives. Nas insists in his freedom to hang out with his "boys," and she and her girlfriends band together. These homosocial bonds tends to reinforce each groups' sense of their relationships with the other sex as oppositional. For instance, she recounts an incident in which the "girlfriends code" provides pressure for her to participate in an assault on one of the friend's boyfriend and the woman he is cheating with. Such strict lines of division reinforce mistrust on each side and minimize the expectation that men and women could socialize across gender lines in ways that were not primarily defined by sex.

Bryan's search for such a relationship is fulfilled in the friendship she develops with Jay-Z. Her narrative of their relationship subverts the paradigms of Baby Mama, groupie, or Vixen as the primary ways by which women relate to men in hip hop culture. Instead she offers a picture of Jay-Z as a caring and considerate friend who allowed her to feel like she was in her "first adult relationship."[37] The adult aspect of their relationship has to do with his perception of her as a peer. Her interest in him is sparked when on their first date, he acknowledges her position in the industry as well as the fact that mothering "is a full time job in itself."[38] Further distinguishing him from Nas, she describes him as emotionally intuitive: "Like an angel in disguise, he always seemed to appear when I needed him the most."[39] Such strategic and contrasting characterizations of Nas's almost parodic notions of masculinity and Jay-Z's sensitivity are central to her self-construction. These distinctions are significant because they reframe the narrative from a salacious account of two men fighting over a sexual prize to an account of how their differing gender politics positioned them in Bryan's affections. Thus, Bryan herself is centered as the subject of the account rather than an object.

They illuminate her effort to balance a commitment to her family relationship with her own need for self-realization. Along with the text's dedication to "all single-mothers" Bryan's strategic self-construction as more than a groupie or Baby Mama suggests her effort to offer a discursive challenge to the hip hop generations' normative understanding of male-female relationships as relationships of financial dependence and emotional separation. The Baby Mama/Baby Daddy relationship parallels the states' call for the restoration of the family to the extent that it links family formation (even informal formations) and economic security. However, as Bryan's narrative illustrates, it also belies the assumption of that call, which is that African American's choose not to marry for moral or cultural reasons, and that the state only reinforces deviant norms by providing benefits to single mothers. Such thinking ignores significant logical contradictions, such as the fact that African American women have historically had less access to cash benefits from the state and would have little reason to purposely elect for dependence on the state over more autonomous routes such as marriage. Moreover, although African American women in the 1950s, 1960s, and 1970s had a higher incidence of babies born outside of wedlock, it is only recently that black women have become lifelong single parents, as they used to marry soon after giving birth. As a phenomenon that gains widespread currency only in the post–civil rights/post-industrial era, we have to understand it as a response to a particular set of socio-economic circumstances, some particulars of which are illuminated in the life writing of hip hop era women.

Each of the texts in examined in this chapter can be seen to engage some important aspects of black women's life writing. Specifically, the oblique engagement of iniquitous social structures through their own subjective experiences connects theses texts to the long history of African American literary production. Their experiences are firmly rooted in the gender and sexual politics of the post–civil rights context. Considering such texts provides a sense of how working-class black women negotiate their subjectivity while facing direct attack from the mainstream media as well as from members of their own social communities. Taking their narratives seriously and on the own terms affirms their attempts to counter these attacks and broadens our perspective of the ways in which black women participate in the analysis of contemporary black life.

NOTES

1. Abramovitz, 34.
2. Ibid., 34.

3. Lisa Duggan, "The New Heteronormativity: The Sexual Politics of Neoliberalism" in *Materializing the New Democracy: Toward a Revitalized cultural Politics*, ed. Russ Castronovo and Dana Nelson (Durham: Duke University Press, 2002), 175–194.

4. Tricia Rose, *The Hip Hop Wars: What We Talk About When We Talk About Hip Hop—and Why it Matters* (New York: Basic Books, 2008).

5. Though many readers remain skeptical of Bush's claims not to have engaged in sex for money, her emphasis on developing the psychological skills necessary to understand the client's desires and cultivate a persona that fulfills the fantasy of those desires without a sexual exchange is consistent with other strippers' accounts.

6. Though Bush is quite celebratory, it is hard to ignore the limits of the opportunities provided by such employment when she describes her own schedule of twelve-hour work shifts, the earnings hierarchy of floor dancers versus VIP room workers or the greater earning potential of the "floor men" (concierge/bouncers).

7. Bush, *Gold Club*, 25.

8. Ibid., 72.

9. Aisha Lockeridge, *Tipping on a Tightrope* (Peter Lang, 2013).

10. Bush, *Gold Club*, 59.

11. Ibid., 59.

12. Ibid., 68.

13. Ibid., 50.

14. Ibid., 113.

15. Ibid., 112.

16. Ibid., 114.

17. Ibid., 112.

18. Some of the best known and most popular from this period include Lily Burana's *Strip City: A Stripper's Farewell Journey Across America* (2001), Elisabeth Eaves' *Bare: The Naked Truth About Stripping* (2004), Lacy Lane's *Confessions of a Stripper* (2004) and *Stripper's Tale: Confessions of a Las Vegas Stripper* (2005) by Diamond.

19. T. Denean Sharpley-Whiting, *Pimps up, Ho's Down*, 145.

20. Neal Gilbert traces out the general trends in welfare policy and perception from the inception of ADC in the 1940s to the most recent reformulation as TANF in his essay, "U.S. Welfare Reform: Rewriting the Social Contract." Of particular interest for the discussion at hand is his observation that "TANF policy revised the essential character of the social safety net provided by U.S. public welfare through the 1990s." This revision reflects the movement of political assumptions away from acceptance of welfare as a social right to an emphasis on recipients' display of social responsibility in order to earn or deserve the support which they receive (386). Such an emphasis on responsibility frames such benefits as a privilege rather than an entitlement as had basically been the case "From the 1960s to the mid-1980s" when according to Gilbert, "the political discourse on welfare was animated by efforts to extend the range of benefits available to the poor."

21. Ibid., 81.

22. Julia Jordan-Zachery, *Black Women, Cultural Images, and Social Policy* (New York: Routledge Books, 2009).

23. Johnnie M. Stover particularly associates this strategy with the spiritual autobiographies by Jarena Lee, Rebecca Cox Jackson and Zilpha X in his study, *Rhetoric and Resistance in Black Women's Autobiography*. Moreover, novelist Tayari Jones makes a provocative comparison of *Confessions* and Harriet Jacobs's *Incidents in the Life of a Slave Girl*.

24. Steffans, *Video Vixen*, 53.

25. Ibid., 96–97.

26. Ibid., 98.

27. Ibid., 108.

28. Ibid., 2–3.

29. Jordan-Zachery, *Black Women*, 94.

30. Teresa Wiltz, "More Confessions of the Video Vixen," *Essence* (October 2005): 270.

31. Bryan, *No Secret*, 16.

32. Ibid., 26.

33. Ibid., 24–25.
34. Ibid., 25.
35. Alexander-Floyd, *Gender, Race, and Nationalism*, 25.
36. Bryan, *No Secret*, 131.
37. Ibid., 136.
38. Ibid., 134.
39. Ibid., 156.

Conclusion

From Critical Practice to Classroom Practice

Throughout this book I have made arguments that affirm the value of a critical reading practice that positions mass fiction as extensive of the traditions we have inherited and which values the interests of consumer audiences. In these final pages I want to address the issue of pedagogy to which all critical practice is, ultimately, tied. Given that aesthetics of popular literature are typically not closely attuned to those of the academy, simply deciding to prioritize mass fictions is but the first step the scholar must take. Once she has made the decision she must confront the task of specifying what aesthetics are at work, if not those to which we are accustomed to paying attention.

Girlfriend fiction and urban fiction create challenges in the classroom since they tend to be more formulaic and emphasize plot and theme over complexity. In these cases, I am guided by the insights of Kristina Graaff. In her essay "Street Literature and the Mode of Spectacular Writing: Popular Fiction between Sensationalism, Education, Politics, and Entertainment" she draws attention to the theatrical nature of street literature, in which the dramatization of the conditions of the "street" are made spectacular. Graaff offers a notion of "spectacular writing" which emphasizes concepts of visibility, immediacy, and externalization of conflicts that can be used to approach this body of writing. What is implied in her argument is the inadequacy of the critical tools with which we commonly approach the study of literature.

The need to "deal with" the direct style of these authors suggests the degree to which we can be invested in the structuralist notion of the author as a figure who renders a singular and objective truth, and, thus, rightfully exercises the role of mediation revealing through the various frameworks of chronology, patterns of language, and psychological interiority act as diagnosis/etiology of the world(s) represented. In this role, then the readers' main job is to receive the message. By contrast, the world of street fiction, as with other popular genres, is much more beholden to the reader as a participant in meaning-making process. In pointing out the moral of the story in advance, the writer draws attention to, rather than obscures, his or her position of power via the narrative. In doing so, the assumption of objectivity embedded in the traditional role of the author is destabilized and the agency of the reader is acknowledged. For example, in the preface to her novella *Unique*, Nikki Turner claims that the purpose of the story is to help its audiences recognize a "hood rat" when they encounter one. In doing so, the author emphasizes her parity with the reader, who, presumably, occupies the same social locale in which such knowledge would be useful or necessary. So the reader and the author are in fact brought together onto the same plane of experience and the specificity of that experience is emphasized over the presumption of universality associated with the traditional authorial perspective. Moreover, the need of the popular author to meet the demands of taste of a specific audience constitutes another form in which power relations are equalized since, in order to sell enough units to be profitable at prices frequently as low as $1.99 for electronic download, authors must keep the objective of meeting those tastes in an uppermost position.

Though Graaff's concept of the spectacular is presented in relation to urban fiction, specifically, it is equally salient for the understanding of Girlfriend fiction, which is also invested in rendering social experiences that resonate directly with its audiences. Though these texts do not highlight the positioning of their authors in the same way that urban fiction does, they do tend to focus on visibility and immediacy in a similar fashion. Particularly, in the emphasis on recognizable character types, social situations, and settings, we can read the authors' attempt to speak to particular audience experiences. Thus, taking a thematic approach to such texts can be valuable for cultivating a sympathetic approach and helping students to see the ways in which this body of literature, while aesthetically distinctive, connects with the conventions and history of various African American literary contexts and endeavors.

To that end, I don't simply engage these texts on sub-generic terms. I use the themes and the characterizations to position contemporary text as coextensive with the canon as it has been formulated. I first implemented this approach with a male authored text, Robert Beck's *Pimp*, and then applied those strategies to my presentation of African American women's literature. Since this experience was central to my rethinking of the relationships among various African American narrative traditions I think it warrants examination here.

Prior to this experiment with *Pimp*, all of my teaching of street lit had been in the context of a course on hip hop culture and literature which, to a certain extent, encouraged a view of the traditions as separate. In the iteration that I am describing, I consciously sought to frame hip hop narrative as coextensive with African American literature, generally. In doing so, I was able to provide a much broader contextualization for hip hop's narrative engagement with themes such as the pursuit of the American Dream, race and economic stratification, and black male visibility; themes with which students are at least somewhat familiar from their reading of traditional black literature.

In this revised course I framed this text as a point of connection between African American oral and literary culture. I began by laying out a sense of the historical relation between African American folklore and literature then introduced students to some specific examples of the bad man figure in the folklore. Instead of insisting though, that the primary relationship of *Pimp* was to the folkloric tradition, I followed the lead provided by Candice Love Jackson's essay, "The Literate Pimp: Robert Beck, Iceberg Slim, and Pimping the African American Novel" and demonstrated the ways in which the text could be read in relation to a more canonical literary tradition. Jackson reads *Pimp*, in particular, as a revision of Ralph Ellison's *Invisible Man*. Ultimately, though, the central question addressed in her essay is actually a crucial one for students of literary studies; in asking us to think about how *Pimp* exceeds the category of autobiography, the examination of the text raises some important questions regarding genre, black canon formation, and contexts of literary production. Guided by this approach, I helped students see how thinking about the text as fictional rather than autobiographical could help us to better understand the historical relationship between black politics and black literature. While the text serves as a cautionary tale whether we see it as pure autobiography or not, pointing out the ways in which Beck frames his narrative in relation to an explicitly literary tradition demonstrates the degree to which political functionality has been a hallmark of the African American literary tradition—a tradition with which the author was clearly familiar.

For instance, I drew attention to the distinctive prose of the text's preface, which is sandwiched between a foreword in which Slim's bottom whore explains that the smell which offends him is that of "[their] nasty whore asses" and the rest of the text proper which presents its supposed illumination of the life in similarly vulgar language. The preface, though, is remarkable for its almost archaic diction and dignified tone, which are reminiscent in style and theme of the apologias commonly associated with the nineteenth century narratives of enslavement. He states: "The account of my brutality and cunning as a pimp will fill many of you with revulsion, however if one intelligent valuable young man or woman can be saved from the destructive slime then the displeasure I have given will have been outweighed by that individual's use of his potential in a socially constructive manner."[1] So in spite of a narrative filled with stories of base exploitation told from a perspective presumably rooted strictly in pimp culture, Beck provides a frame which destabilizes the norms of that culture and aligns himself with the an activist tradition of letters within the black community.

Armed with the framework of the folkloric tradition of the bad man whose badness is motivated by the racial boundaries imposed in a racist society, students were able to articulate quite eloquently how Beck's work offers a familiar critique of a racially divided society and the ways in which it challenges black male invisibility. Thus, this text allowed us to think critically about the interrelationship of hip hop, the folkloric tradition, and canonical literature. In doing so, then, Beck's text raises the question of the politics of black community out of which he writes. The framework I erected for examining this question of historical context utilized the scaffolding of the black public sphere. Here I incorporated an overview of Holloway House publishing company and put it in the context of larger shifts in black political discourse away from physical segregation in the rural south, to economic segregation in the nation's urban centers.

In working with the literature of contemporary African American women, an important part of my approach has been to place some of the new archetypes I've identified in this study—such as the Bitch or the Diva—in dialogue with more traditional images of black femininity such as the blues woman. For instance, I have taught Vickie Stringer's *Let That Be the Reason* in a unit with Alice Walker's *The Color Purple* and a chapter from Angela Davis's *Blues Legacies and Black Feminism*. Doing so allows for a rich conversation regarding the variety of narrative forms that constitute the African American literary tradition, the changing same of black vernacular speech, and the politics of representing black women in the public sphere. In other cases, I have paired Nella Larsen's *Quicksand* with Sista Souljah's *The Coldest Winter Ever* or Heidi Durrow's *The Girl Who Fell From the Sky* to compare the nature of black women's quests for social and sexual power at either end of the twentieth century and to consider how notions of racial identification compare in these distinctive eras. In presenting these texts as they connect, I felt enabled to participate in the very important work of reconnecting the African American canon as it has been (re)constructed since the 1980s with the reading tastes of mass audiences outside of the academy.

Teaching such a variety of texts requires that we pay close attention to social contextualization, but to a great extent, this is always the case for African American literature. However, in certain contexts, I think the need for such attention is more pronounced. If, as I have argued, above the specific tastes and social norms of such a uniquely defined audience shape the aesthetics of street fiction, what happens when such literature is taken up in the contexts in which many of us teach—in university settings in which our classrooms are dominated by middle- to upper-class white students from fairly homogenous class and racial geographic locales? As Kristina Graaff argues, there is great potential "that the novels' hypervisuality, vulgarity and lack of subtlety lead to a degradation of black literary fiction and the reinscription of racist stereotypes" (12).

This insight is particularly useful in thinking about how to deal with questions of sexuality—its graphic representation and the tendency for it to be transactionalized—in urban fiction. It is easy for students to condemn the actions of the characters and judge them rather harshly. In my experience teaching Vickie Stringer's *Let That Be the Reason*, for instance, students have pointed out that the character's professed commitment to her son and his well-being is belied by any real extended development of their relationship in the text. In dealing with this tendency to judge the characters, I emphasize two factors: 1) How such a reaction obscures the very critiques that arise in these novels and 2) the intervention into hip hop representations that is accomplished by making those critiques from a specifically gendered position.

To bring these issues to the fore, I draw on an overview of female types identified and critiqued by Gwendolyn Pough's reading of filmic "girls in the hood" which contrasts male authored representations which rely on a rigid typology of black femininity with the more fully developed images that contextualize certain stereotypical behaviors in the characters.[2] I then ask students to consider how the main character's pursuit of her ambitions (which are in and of themselves consistent with a mainstream American ethos) exceeds the stereotypes and raises complex questions about the gender and racial double standards. In focusing on the resistance the character encounters to her attempt to move from working in the sex industry to the more lucrative and in her own estimation less demeaning drug trade, students are able to identify a stratification that mirrors that of the most conservative corporate environment to the extent that it sees women as fundamentally unsuited for some roles on the basis of their biology. The novel dramatizes in spectacular fashion some of the forms that working-class women's ambitions may take according to the perceived possibilities of that social milieu. Moreover, as it demonstrates some of the obstacles they face due to sexism, it reveals the alignment of those aspirations with the American dream and its fundamental conservatism.

While teaching street lit can be a challenging proposition, I have found that such texts also provide significant boons for teaching. The first is that most students actually complete the readings, and they read in an active way, engaging the characters and actions with passion. This provides a platform from which the teacher can fruitfully engage the much larger social issues contained in such work and also demonstrate the diversity of writing dealing with African American subjects.

By contrast, while "Girlfriend" and other mass fiction forms present fewer challenges in terms of the presentation of sexuality and stereotypes of criminality, they do present a challenge in terms of their address of a highly particular social experience. Students may find it difficult to connect with the experiences of the middle-class and middle-aged African American women that populate these texts. In this case, I find that emphasizing extra-textual issues such as the politics of canon formation provides a point of connection for the student of American literature. In these cases I focus on issues of critical reception and the historical construction of female subjectivity. Using essays like Calvin Hernton's "The Sexual Mountain and Black Women Writers," or Mary Helen Washington's "The Darkened Eye Restored" helps to establish a historical perspective of the difficulty African American women have faced in carving out an affirmative space in African American literary history. Thus, even if students do not identify directly with the experiences representing they are able to see this significance of such narratives in broad context.

Examining work by Terry McMillan has enabled productive conversations about what a term like popular literature even means. Hers is a case where one can discuss how sales, audience identification, means of publication and theme are all factors which impact the classification and scholarly reception of a text. I discuss her career as an example that illustrates many of the contradictions of classification; describing how her self-published novel *Mama*, was initially well received because of its exploration of single motherhood. We talk about how this thematic made for an easier alliance with the canonical tradition since it was consistent with an established sense of black literary politics. However, the enormous success of *Waiting to Exhale*, shifted the perception of her work to the realm of popular, and it was deemed unworthy of scholarly attention. However marginalized McMillan's work was in the academy, its impact on the publishing industry's willingness to invest in narratives by black women is undeniable. Emphasizing the politics of publishing allows students who have never experienced a lack of access to "black books" to get some sense of what a recent development this is and to see how it has enabled the landscape in which they live. When possible, I link McMillan's story to those of contemporary figures like Wahida Clark and Vickie Stringer to suggest how their opportunities are simultaneously enabled by the success of Girlfriend fiction in the late twentieth century and by the popularity of hip hop based representations.

Taking the challenge presented by black women's popular fiction offers many potential rewards. Foremost among them, in my opinion, is the opportunity to reconnect black literary scholarship and black collectivity. At present, there is more separation between the critical and creative spheres as well as a notable chasm between black academics and working-class black communities than at any other time in history. As Reggie Scott Young notes in "Theoretical Influences and Experimental Resemblances," "Unlike students who used to receive an education in Black Studies, critics today are no longer encouraged to view the black community as a classroom where they might learn valuable lesson about the very texts they seek to explicate."[3] The lack of social coherence among African Americans necessitates the conscious examination of our critical practice since as individuals we may be working from a singular perspective. By developing an expansive critical practice that incorporates the sensibilities of the reading public, we take an important step toward assuaging anxieties regarding the viability of African American literature. And, we can put paid to Young's charge that: "today the field seems to lack recognized scholars who are entrusted to define the central goals and concerns of African American literary studies in the early twenty-first century."[4]

NOTES

1. Iceberg Slim, *Pimp: The Story of My Life* (Cash Money Content, 2011) (original publication date 1969), Preface.
2. Gwendolyn Pough, *Check it While I Wreck it: Black Womanhood: Hip Hop Culture and the Public Sphere*.
3. Young, 22.
4. Young, 23.

Bibliography

Abramovitz, Mimi. "Theorising the Neoliberal State for Social Work." In *The Sage Handbook of Social Work.* ed. Mel Gray, James Midgley, Stephen Webb, 2012.

Alexander-Floyd, Nikol. *Gender, Race, and Nationalism in Contemporary Black Politics.* New York: Palgrave Macmillan, 2007.

Ansa, Tina McElroy. *You Know Better.* New York: William Morrow, 2002.

———. *The Hand I Fan With.* New York: Anchor Books, 1996.

Ashe, Bertram. "Theorizing the Post-Soul Aesthetic: An Introduction." *African American Review* 41, no. 4 (2007): 609–623.

Baker, Houston. "Critical Memory and the Black Public Sphere." In *The Black Public Sphere: A Public Culture Book.* ed. The Black Public Sphere Collective, 7–37. Chicago: The University of Chicago Press, 1995.

Baldwin, Davarian. "Black Empires, White Desires: The Spatial Politics of Identification in the Age of Hip Hop." In *That's The Joint: the Hip Hop Studies Reader.* ed. Murray Forman and Mark Anthony Neal. New York: Routledge, 2004.

Beavers, Herman. "African American Women Writers and Popular Fiction: Theorizing Black Womanhood." *The Cambridge Companion to African American Women's Literature.* ed. Angelyn Mitchell and Danielle K. Taylor. New York: Cambridge University Press, 2009.

Bobo, Jacqueline. *Black Women as Cultural Readers.* New York: Columbia University Press, 1995.

Bryan, Carmen. *It's No Secret: From Nas to Jay-Z, From Seduction to Scandal—A Hip Hop Helen of Troy Tells All.* New York: VH1 Books, 2006.

Bush, Jacklyn "Diva." *The Gold Club: How I Went From Gold Room to Court Room.* Los Angeles: Milligan Books, 2003.

Cain, Chelsea. "You Go on a Diet, Girl!" *New York Times*, July 24, 2005.

Campbell, Bebe Moore. *72 Hour Hold.* New York: Anchor Books, 2006.

———. "Black Books Are Good for Business." In *Defining Ourselves: Black Writers in the 90s.* ed. Elizabeth Nunez and Brenda Greene. New York: Peter Lang Publishing, 1999.

Chiles, Nick. "Their Eyes Were Reading Smut."

Clark, Wahida. *Every Thug Needs a Lady.* New York: Dafina/Kensington, 2006.

———. *Thugs and the Women Who Love Them.* New York: Kensington Publishing, 2005.

Collins, Patricia Hill. *From Black Power to Hip Hop: Racism, Nationalism, and Feminism.* Philadelphia: Temple University Press, 2006.

———. *Black Sexual Politics: African Americans, Gender, and the New Racism.* New York: Routledge, 2005.

Dubey, Madhu. *Black Women Novelists and the Nationalist Aesthetic.* Bloomington and Indianapolis: Indiana University Press, 1994.

duCille, Ann. *The Coupling Convention: Sex, Text, and Tradition in Black Women's Fiction.* New York: Oxford University Press, 1993.

Duggan, Lisa. "The New Heteronormativity: The Sexual Politics of Neoliberalism." In *Materializing the New Democracy: Toward a Revitalized Cultural Politics*, ed. Russ Castronovo and Dana Nelson. (Durham: Duke University Press, 2002): 175–194.

Epstein, Cynthia Fuchs and Stephen R. Duncombe. "Women Clerical Workers." In *Dual City: Restructuring New York*. ed. John Mollenkopf and Manuel Castells, (New York: Russell Sage Foundation, 1991): 177–203.

Franklin, Donna L. *Ensuring Inequality: The Structural Transformation of the African-American Family.* New York: Oxford University Press, 1997.

———. *What's Love Got to Do with It? Understanding and Healing the Rift between Black Men and Women.* New York: Simon & Schuster, 2000.

Gates, Henry Louis Jr. *The Signifying Monkey: A Theory of African-American Literary Criticism.* New York: Oxford University Press, 1988.

Gilbert, Sandra M. and Susan Gubar. *The Madwoman in the Attic: The Woman Writer and the Nineteenth-Century Literary Imagination.* New Haven and London: Yale University Press, 1979.

Gilroy, Paul. *Against Race: Imagining Political Culture Beyond the Color Line.* Cambridge, Massachusetts: The Belknap Press of Harvard University Press, 2001.

Giovanni, Nikki. "Nikki-Rosa." in *The Norton Anthology of African American Literature.* ed. Henry Louis Gates Jr. and Nellie Y. McKay. New York: W.W. Norton & Company, 1997.

Griffin, Farah Jasmine. "That the Mothers May Soar and the Daughters May Know Their Names: A Retrospective of Black Feminist Literary Criticism." *Signs: Journal of Women in Culture and Society* 32, no. 2 (2007): 483–507.

Goyal, Yogita. "The Gender of Diaspora in *Tar Baby.*" *Modern Fiction Studies* 52, no. 2 (2006): 393–414.

hooks, bell. *Communion: The Female Search for Love.* New York: William Morrow, 2002.

Harris-Perry, Melissa. *Sister Citizen: Shame, Stereotypes, and Black Women in America.* New Haven and London: Yale University Press, 2011.

Herman, David, et al. *Narrative Theory: Core Concepts and Critical Debates.* Columbus: The Ohio State University Press, 2012.

Jones, Lisa. *Bulletproof Diva: Tales of Race, Sex, and Hair.* New York: Anchor Books, 1994.

Jordan-Zachery, Julia S. *Black Women, Cultural Images, and Social Policy.* New York: Routledge Books, 2009.

Keyes, Cheryl. "Empowering Self, Making Choices, Creating Spaces: Black Female Identity via Rap Music Performance." In *That's The Joint: the Hip-Hop Studies Reader.* ed. Murray Forman and Mark Anthony Neal. New York: Routledge, 2004.

Levine, Lawrence. *Highbrow/Lowbrow: The Emergence of Cultural Hierarchy in America.* Cambridge, Massachusetts: Harvard University Press, 1988.

Lockridge, Aisha. *Tipping on a Tightrope: Divas in African American Literature.* New York: Peter Lang, 2012.

Marshall, Elizabeth, Jeanine Staples, and Simone Gibson. "Ghetto Fabulous: Reading Black Adolescent Femininity in Contemporary Urban Street Fiction." *Journal of Adolescent and Adult Literacy* 53, no. 1 (2009): 28–36.

McLaughlin, Thomas. *Street Smarts and Critical Theory: Listening to the Vernacular.* Madison: University of Wisconsin Press, 1996.

McMillan, Terry. *The Interruption of Everything.* New York: Signet Books, 2006.

Morgan, Joan. *When Chickenheads Come Home to Roost: A Hip Hop Feminist Breaks it Down.* New York: Simon and Schuster, 1999.

Murray, Victoria. "Triple Crown Winner." *Black Issues Book Review.* May–June 2014, 28.

Neal, Larry. "The Black Arts Movement." 1968. In *Within the Circle: An Anthology of African American Literary Criticism from the Harlem Renaissance to the Present.* ed. Angelyn Mitchell, 184-198. Durham: Duke University Press, 1994.

Neal, Mark Anthony. *New Black Man.* New York: Routledge, 2006.

———. *Soul Babies: Black Popular Culture and the Post-Soul Aesthetic.* New York: Routledge, 2002.

———. *What the Music Said: Black Popular Music and Black Public Culture*. New York: Routledge, 1999.

Pate, Alexs. *In the Heart of the Beat: The Poetry of Rap*. Lanham, Maryland: Scarecrow Press, 2010.

Pereira, Malin Walther. "Periodizing Toni Morrison's Work from The Bluest Eye to Jazz." *MELUS* 22, no. 3 (1997): 71–82.

Phillips, Deborah. *Women's Fiction 1945-2005: Writing Romance*. London: Continuum Books, 2006.

Rambsy, Howard. *The Black Arts Enterprise and the Production of African American Poetry*. Ann Arbor: The University of Michigan Press, 2011.

Richards, Paulette. *Terry McMillan: A Critical Companion*. West Port, Connecticut: Greenwood Press, 1999.

Rogers, Mary. *Novels, Novelists, and Readers: Toward a Phenomenological Sociology of Literature*. New York: State University of New York Press, 1991.

Rose, Tricia. *The Hip Hop Wars: What We Talk About When We Talk About Hip Hop—and Why It Matters*. New York: Basic Books, 2008.

———. *Black Noise: Rap Music and Black Culture in Contemporary America*. Hanover: University Press of New England, 1994.

Sharpley-Whiting, T. Denean. *Pimps Up, Ho's Down: Hip Hop's Hold on Young Black Women*. New York: New York University Press, 2007.

Steffans, Karinne. *Confessions of a Video Vixen*. New York: Amistad, 2006.

Stringer, Vicki. *Let That Be the Reason*. New York: Atria Books, 2009.

Taylor, Paul C. "Post Black, Old Black." *African American Review* 41, no. 4 (2007): 625–640.

Thaggert, Miriam. "Marriage, Moynihan, *Mahagony*: Success and the Post-Civil Rights Black Female Professional in Film." *American Quarterly* 64, no. 4 (2012): 715–740.

Washington, Mary Helen. "The Darkened Eye Restored: Notes Toward a Literary History of Black Women." In *Within the Circle: An Anthology of African American Literary Criticism from the Harlem Renaissance to the Present*. ed. Angelyn Mitchell, 442–453. Durham: Duke University Press, 1994.

Williams, Dana A. "Contemporary African American Women Writers." *The Cambridge Companion to African American Women's Literature*. ed. Angelyn Mitchell and Danille K. Taylor, 71–86. New York: Cambridge University Press, 2009.

Wiltz, Teresa. "More Confessions of the Video Vixen." *Essence*, October 2005, 270.

Wyatt, Jean. "Patricia Hill Collins's *Black Sexual Politics* and the Genealogy of the Strong Black Woman." *Studies in Gender and Sexuality* 9, no.1 (2008): 52–67.

Young, Reggie. "Theoretical Influences and Experimental Resemblances: Ernest J. Gaines and Recent Critical Approaches to the Study of African American Fiction." In *Contemporary African American Fiction: New Essays*. ed. Dana A. Williams, 11–36. Columbus: Ohio University Press, 2009.

Index

About the Author

Beauty Bragg is associate professor in the Department of English and Rhetoric at Georgia College and State University, where she also contributes courses in women's studies and Africana studies. Her essays and book chapters on contemporary African American literature and diaspora literature are published in *Palimpsest: A Journal on Women, Gender and the Black International; Literary Expressions of African Spirituality,* and *Percival Everett: Writing Other/Wise.*

AUG 2 3 2019

CPSIA information can be obtained
at www.ICGtesting.com
Printed in the USA
LVHW080442090819
627064LV00006B/183/P